If they have never met you, how can they say those awful things about you?

Now that I have seen you, I can tell them all that you are more beautiful than I could ever have imagined.

To Sigered and all his forgotten children.

CONTENTS

INTRODUCTION

The Stour is an East Anglian river and is pronounced like *door* as often as it is like *hour*. The origins of her name are obscure, but likely mean "strong" or "powerful".

Her beginnings are gentle though, her mother county is Cambridgeshire where the river finds the light of day at Wratting Common just a few miles from the Suffolk border. The latter county has her as its own for few short miles more, before a third shire comes to claim its share. By the time the Stour reaches Essex, she has already been in flow for six or seven miles.

This splendid river rolls east in increasingly fluvial splendour, passing predominantly through flat or softly undulating countryside and by quiet villages. In places she is so filled with visual delight she has caused more than one artist to set up an easel and capture her for the ages.

Through lazy mental reference, and the fact that the Stour's most famous son, John Constable, hailed from the northern bank of the river, she is more often associated with that county. For most of her life. though, the Stour is a shared river, passing occasionally from Essex to Suffolk or vice versa for a moment's safe-keeping, but usually holding hands with both of her favourite aunts until she reaches her destiny in the eastern sea.

This book is all about the right bank of that famous river, in the county of seaxes. A series of walks take us from a bridge near Water Hall in New England, to a jetty in Harwich, with so much in between, all the time with the river on our left.

This is the story of a river, the Stour, an *Essex* river.

An Explanation.....

When writing a book of walks, one is always in a quandary as to who to cater for, especially when the walk is A to B rather than circular. How do you get to the place you are starting from? Where do you leave your car? How do you get back to it? Do you even use your car at all? Does one presume that you live locally and will pick one of the walks and return home by car, perhaps returning for another when the mood suits?

This book is written as a journey from the source of the Essex Stour to the place where it finds the sea. This is some fifty-odd miles and (hopefully) caters for all of the above.

The main narrative is one of a carless journey (excluding one or two possible taxis) using public transport as much as possible, presuming the reader is not local and walking the whole thing in four days. However, there are also tips about how the days can be more and shorter.

There are also tips about where you might stay.

Of course, you can always find a way to leave your car somewhere – and (via taxi, train or bus) walk your way back to it; and if you live nearby you can just drive on home (or get the train of course).

The walk is generally west to east, which creates problems when drawing maps on portrait-orientated pages. For that reason, most of the more detailed maps are swung around 90 degrees, with east facing the top.

Key

 **Point of Interest**

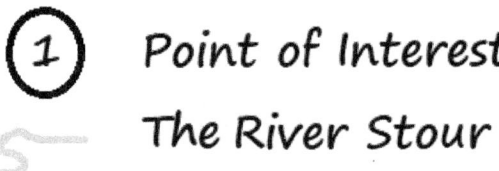 **The River Stour**

 **The Chosen Path**

Day One – From near Water Hall to Sudbury (12 miles)

Two-day short walk option, staying in Clare (Suffolk)

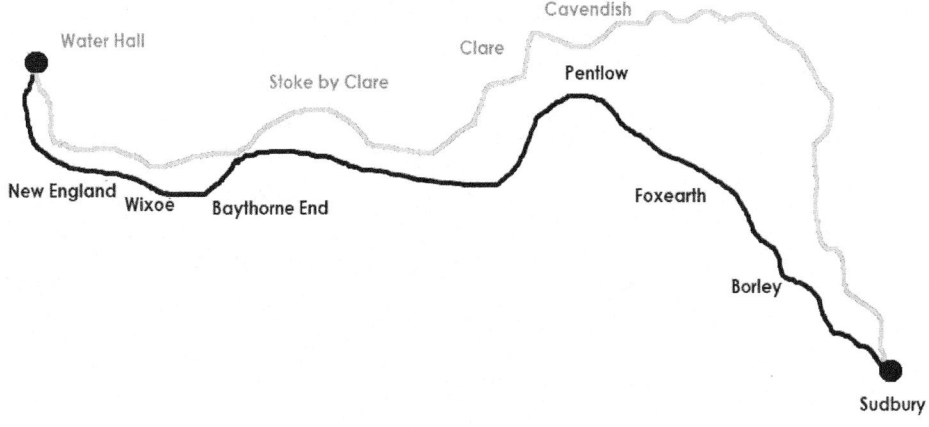

Day one takes us from the beginning to the first town of any size on the Stour (Sudbury, with a population of about 15,000).

It is a landscape of flat and rolling pasture, scarcely touching any settlements in the early stages and is pepper-potted with sumptuous country houses. Some of the early parts are dominated by verge-walking along the A1017, then Ashen Road, before the fields come in to their own.

The middle stages veer somewhat away from the river itself. To stay as close to the Stour as possible would make this walk very long (and would not allow you to actually see much of the river in any event). But this middle and later stretch are the realm of some lovely churches and villages.

Because of the predominantly rural nature of this part of northern Essex (much more rural than the county to the north) the choices of places to sleep are limited. That is why the walk ends up just over the border in Sudbury, the town of Thomas Gainsborough.

Day One - Part One

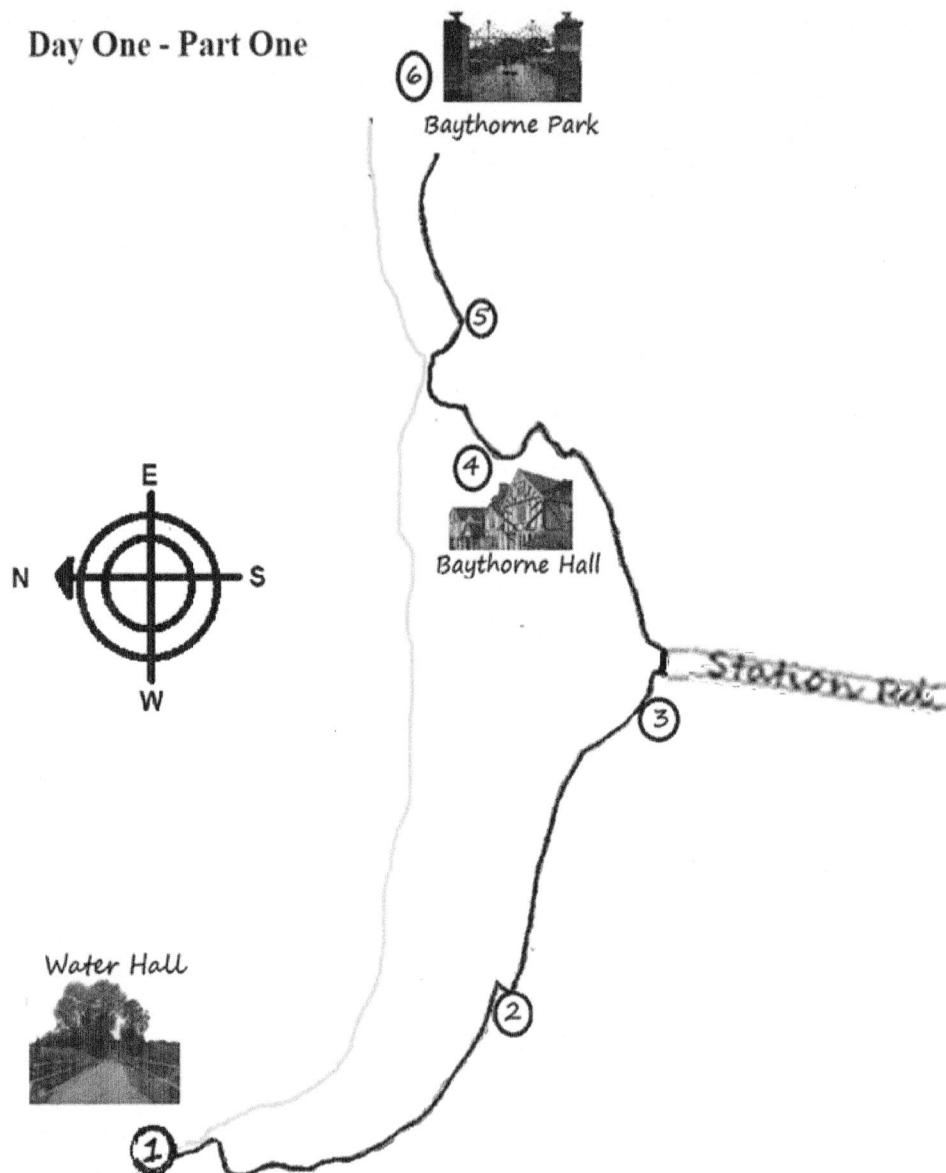

Baythorne Park

Baythorne Hall

Station Rd.

Water Hall

E
N — S
W

The beginning of the journey is not straightforward, not as easy as parking your car or catching a bus and then beginning at "x" with a well-trodden path, far from it. The opening exchanges are messy and involve (perhaps literally if you take a wrong turn) hacking through the long grass until the soft meadow can be felt underfoot. It involves being some distance away from the watercourse itself at times, walking narrow verge-ways and occasionally having to contend with traffic on narrow lanes. But, when all is done, it brings its own rewards.

GETTING THERE:

The Beestons Bus service from Sudbury to Haverhill (taking in Sturmer – near to the start of the walk) has been axed and only partially replaced (going as far as Clare), by Chambers.

It is possible to combine two different buses (changing and waiting at Clare, lovely but adding much to the day) which may prove irksome. If you do choose this, the options are very limited, with buses leaving Clare War Memorial at 08:10, 09:30, 12:00 and 15:20 and discharging you at Linnets Lane some 13 minutes later. From here, turnabout and head south on a grass verge next to a field on the left and in 200 metres you will meet up with the description below. In all candour, it is better to get a taxi (details at the back of the book).

Aim for just south of Sturmer on the A1017, quoting "Waterhall Lane". About 50 metres south of the road sign for Sturmer (on one of those white field gate signs) is a sign advertising Waterhall Kennels & Cattery. Opposite is the large, cream-coloured multi-ranged pile of Pitt House.

This is close to a large oak and a turning for a little lane which is signed, "Unsuitable for heavy goods vehicles." Your fare paid for, that little lane is where it all begins.

About a hundred metres down there is a little bridge (#1). To the left, all is Suffolk, over the bridge likewise. Over to your right though, (at least the nearest half), that is where the shire of the East Saxon begins. In fact, much of the land over to your left was originally in Sigered's realm (he was the last king of Essex by the way), but has overtime been transferred to Suffolk, and that isn't the only occasion this has happened, as we shall see on our journey.

The beginning

Google Street images show a bunch of bare-chested types sitting and having a drink on the nearby path, whilst others fish and try their luck. Nonesuch were in evidence though as the journey proper began. About turn and there is a short stretch of path tracing the river and the border, the ideal scenario for a walk of that very description. However, after about 70 metres, this is brought to a sudden end. Another bridge, narrow, wooden, hand-rails, pedestrian only. This leads to the other side, the wrong side for our purposes. Whilst it is physically possible to follow the watery strand a little further, it irresistibly leads to a tangle of bush, shrub and private land which means the third bridge is the end of all hope. Not for the last time, you will find yourself in a place you should not be, disappointed by the fact that the river, or at least easy access to it – something which feels like an inalienable right - is denied by the private ownership of some well-to-do, lucky type. By all means enjoy the extra bit of riverside walking, but do not seek to trespass.

If wishing to avoid a "there and back" detour for the enjoyment of just a little bit of river, the best thing is to turn right at the second bridge (that narrow, wooden one) and head back towards the A1017. Fifty metres on is an opening in the hedge, a black public footpath finger sign, and your first bit of traffic dodging.

This is by no means the worst of such instances, and indeed for a while the verges on both sides are wide enough to walk unhindered. The right-hand-side has it though, especially if two-abreast. 100 metres on, past a pair of houses, Meadow View and Maple House a 1960s concrete-roofed steep-pitched chalet-bungalow/Tudorbethan timbered gable mash-up.

Hereabouts though, the overhanging trees seek to reclaim the pathway and safe passage is best achieved by crossing back to the left. Now is a side-street, the private Fordwater Close, containing four bungalows and the waterworks. The latter is caged off, the former can be accessed to give a thirty-metres distant, through-some-trees view of the Stour (so not worth it). We move on, the wide verge narrows to nothing, so a crossing back over to the right is necessary and we go past a field gate with concrete hardstanding leading to stabling in the distance. The verge path now tucks in and is sheltered from the road by a band of trees, relief for the two dwellings including the oddly-mansarded Scotch Cottage and the metal-gated home of "Unique 27 Chauffeurs."

The shelter from the traffic is soon gone and the re-emergence on to the A1017 shows slim pickings verge-wise, though still usable, as one passes over Wastoe Bridge which crosses a small tributary of the mother river. Back to the left-hand side for less danger, with more open land to the left and the village sign for New England bids our four-wheel friends to cut their speed (often to no avail!).

The Stour now is 250 metres to our left, not even a sniff, no way of cutting through for a glimpse. The next point of reference is the commercial premises of Cut Maple Fires & Stoves ("Trade and Public Welcome"), followed by a currently unused premises ("To Let") before the comfort of the walled -in tarmac gives way to the roadside again where, there is at least now, a hardened footway.

A string of houses on the left, first up the charmingly-appointed Elstree, then the more modern, but gated The Beeches, next the equally charming, but un-treed and starkly-gravelled The Elms. Now the small pink headquarters, preponderance of vehicles and the ramshackle outbuildings and general disarray of Colne Valley Motors.

Turn your eyes to the right though, and there my friends is a public house – The Birdbrook Tavern (#2) – and early temptation to salve. Formerly the Taste of China, and before that Colne Valley Arms, this was nearing completion in its restoration during an early scouting mission and the owners kindly let me park up as I attempted to way-find this particular section – thank you The Birdbrook Tavern. For hire as a venue, it is planning to become once more a pub – so watch this space!

The Birdbrook Tavern

If you can resist this, a sharp turn left (with CVM on your left) and 200 metres later, you are at the Stour! This is a pleasant enough stretch, 400 metres of glimpsed shining water, the odd cantankerous goose, but at the end of it, by a wooden bridge with glimpses across the river to the outbuildings of Wixoe Mill, I was asked where I had come from "the pub" I explained, which was technically correct. I was advised, by the young woman with her brood, that the bit where the grass was mown (i.e. all the way around the edges) was all private. The upshot is, that this section is not to be walked. It was unclear what was private and what was not, and to be honest, the views were not too spectacular (until the end).

So....cross over to the pub. Eat, drink or whatever, and having done what you need to, follow the road on, briefly vulnerable to the traffic, but crossing the field ditch and taking a path along the field edge, with the A1017 and the forbidden fields to your left.

This path, albeit between 100 and 250 metres from the source of our desire, is one of the most straightforward elements of the early part of the journey and goes for almost 2km.

Eventually, though, it arrives at a junction (#3), with a sign pointing us right to Birdbrook (which, incidentally, is near to the source of the River Colne, but that is another journey). This is Station Road, and with the briefest of excursions to the right (50 metres), past a pair of cottages and a tatty shed, the next bit of "easy" presents itself as a footpath finger sign urges us left. The way it points almost indicates we should go across the middle of the field, but a friendlier (to the farmer) route is to follow the well-trodden path behind those two cottages now called Hunnex Green and the next dwelling Rosemary Cottage (whose names I discerned by erroneously taking a walk in front of them on a dangerous roadside attempt). This takes you close to the gardens of those properties, very close and the signage (and busy hens) urge you to move on by.

This path continues just over 1km, and if you wish to avoid walking on crops gets thinner and thinner until a 20 metre stretch which is fairly perilous. It appears a route may be possible, tucking behind a bunch of trees and through some farm buildings and it is by no means clear whether this is private, so the choices are between that or the 20-metre peril.

The trial over with, a thin grass path appears on the left. This passes a most stunning Tudor house, home to Baythorne Wines. This is Baythorne Hall (#4), an uncelebrated Grade I listed architectural gem which has been tree ring-dated to 1341, though improved in the 16th and 20th centuries. This is the home of the Unwin family which runs the wine shop, as well as a cookery school. Sadly Baythorne Hall is not open to the public. Well, the house isn't, but....a sign on a cob wall alerts us to Tarka's café. Just a few yards on is a car park, a hop over the fence, rather than walking the hundred odd metres to the official entrance (and back), we're in.

A hop over the fence is recommended!

Baythorne Hall

I stop for a drink at Tarka's (serious point – strong coffee is a bad idea, from this point there will not be a toilet <u>forever</u>) and I ask if the river can be accessed (not for that, for viewing – there is a WC at Tarka's by the way).

Tarka's

The waitress points to the French doors at the back of the building and these take me to a fenced in area with lawn, raised beds and some sort of toy tractor for kids to drive around on. By failing to enter this area and squeezing through the gap not for wider people, between the fence and a tree, I find the Stour again, just 60 metres away. And what a lovely stretch! Still, but not be-algaed waters, trees overhanging and dipping their heads for a sip, ornamentally-shaped wooden benches; reeds and ducks, numbered pegs which represent what? Berths for tying boats? More likely for fishing from. Lilly pads float on the glassy water, all is most well, but soon must end.

Again the Stour!

200 metres on and we must turn right and hug the edge of the provident field (I had probed further along, through a mess of undergrowth and found a boggy area, and what look like a drainage ditch or tributary, either way it was a difficult one until I found again a private garden with a tennis court and all and was reminded of my earlier mistake). Anyway, that field edge brings us to the exit from lovely Baythorne Hall and the road must be crossed to the right and the verge walked for 200 metres.

This becomes increasingly steep, although there is room. The land at the top has been recently fenced in by the owner, and bears a "welcome to the country" sign of "Dogs Loose" nice. The fence very slightly reduces the space available for walking and stops you sneaking behind the trees – but at least gives you something to cling on to.

As you reach the end of this precipitous verge, you will notice the sign for Baythorne End and will need to cross just as you reach a gault brick building which was a pub, and indeed carries the name "The Swan" (#5).

As you cross over left, there is, thank God, a pavement outside yet another steeply-pitched chalet bungalow, this one called Hall Cottage. Then is Burleigh House, an attractive old stock cottage which invites you around the corner, with a teasing prospect of the river just up Mill Road. But no. Having reached the river, there is a stub path of just a couple of metres, which leads to a gate and private land. By all means linger and look at the river, but the righteous path is across from Burleigh House, past a multi -fingered sign telling you of Clare, Long Melford, Wixoe and the Colne Valley Steam Railway, and now along Ridgewell Road until a gravelled path veers off to the left, where an old concrete footpath sign has been recently emblazoned with the "Stour Valley Path" logo and leads you to a pedestrian gate through Baythorne Park (#6).

At times the vehicular gates are also open, but either way we're in. This is the first time we've encountered the Stour Valley Path (SVP), which began back near Newmarket and continues all the way to Cattawade, opposite Manningtree, and crosses the river and the border several times.

Incidentally, Wikipedia contends that this is a "60-mile long distance footpath in Suffolk", erm, I don't think so. Airbrushing the southernmost of those sister counties from reference? *Naughty* Wikipedia. Anyway, the SVP was opened in 1994 and is celebrating its Silver Jubilee.

Day One Part Two

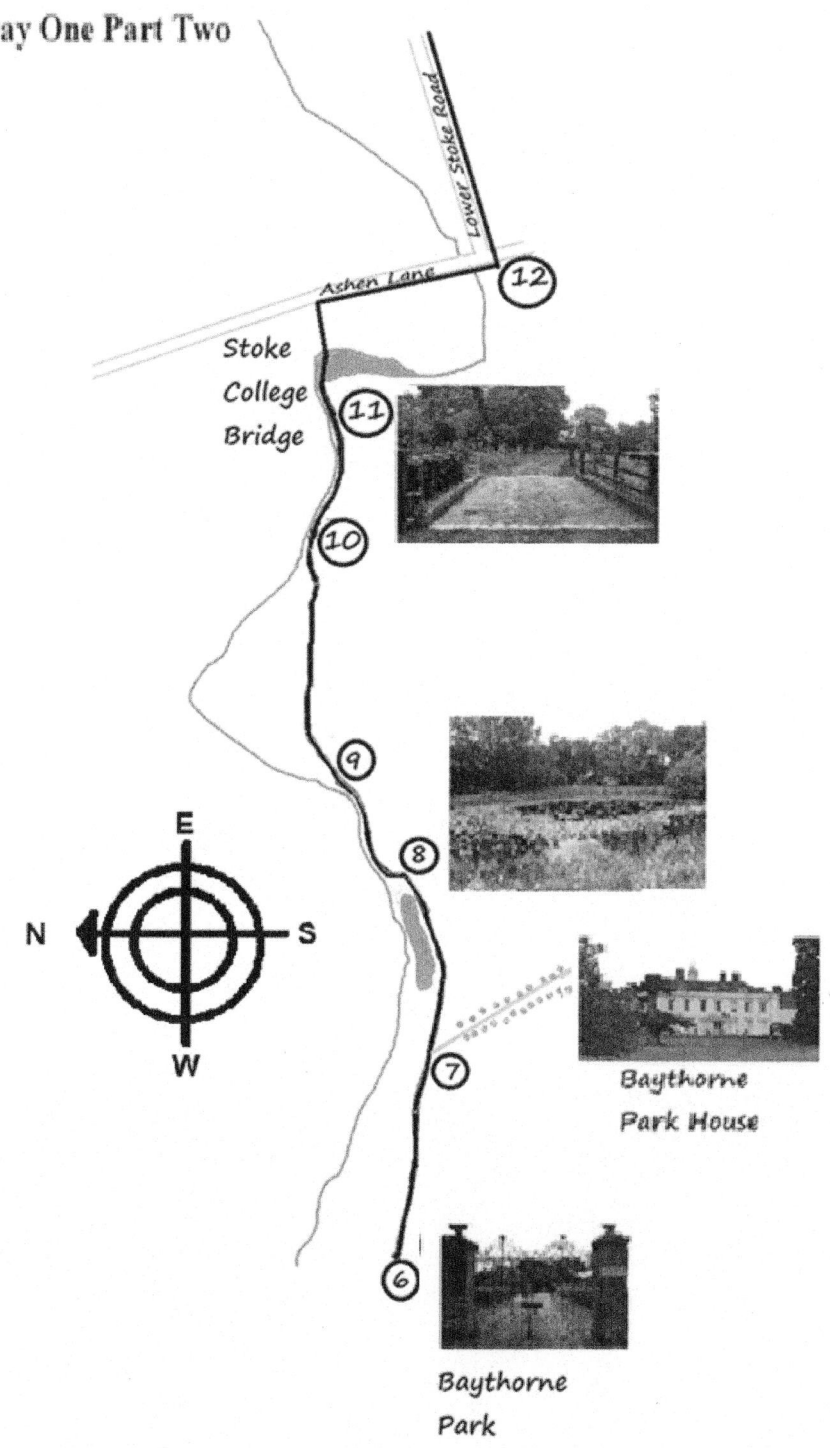

Lower Stoke Road

Ashen Lane

⑫

Stoke
College
Bridge

⑪

⑩

⑨

⑧

⑦

Baythorne
Park House

⑥

Baythorne
Park

E
N S
W

The first part of the Baythorne Park journey passes by cream/white rendered houses (two to the right, one to the left) and then sees a 300 - metre stretch along an avenue of mature trees. At the end of this (just after a sign advising of guard dogs) is a clear sign pointing you to the left as the avenue swings around to the right (#7). It's worth lingering just a moment though to see the impressive Baythorne Park framed between the lines of trees which stretch for half a kilometre.

Remembering that this is private property and you are on a public right of way (over which you may "pass and repass", but certainly not hang around) it is time to move away from the impressive building and edge over a stile towards our watery desire.

Impressive, but Private - Turn Left Here..

Cows chew the cud here, and in the calving season may be left well alone. A curious youngster walked towards me (apparently when cattle come towards you they are being "curious", this makes them no less frightening in my estimation, they may appear docile, but they are <u>massive</u>), but I shooed it away, not wanting mother - or any of her sixteen sisters - to feel the need to come over and supervise. Hanging a quick right, follow the path along and away from the beef and after a couple of hundred metres, there is an exquisite ornamental pond (#8), itself a hundred metres long and not to be confused with the Stour, which is just the other side of it. Next to it is a folly, most charming and typical of this part of the country, north Essex and south Suffolk where there appears to be a disproportionate amount of fine properties. Way over to the right is a clearer view of the magnificent Baythorne Park, still requiring a zoom lens for any decent detail.

This Grade II listed building, in a 676-acre holding, including 48 acres of parkland, was built by George Pyke in 1668. Subsequent owners include one King Viall, who was not a king at all, that was just his name. The house and grounds were most recently in the news in 2017 when they were on sale for some £11 million.

When the pond is done, another stile presents itself with the SVP logo emblazoned and soon we are in the thick of a wood, with the Stour gently gurgling and occasionally visible over to our left (always the left).

The wood, no more than thirty metres wide, is about 200 metres long. This then ends at a stile and we break out into the open. Here, just feet away on the, well you know which side, is the lovely Stour, shallow, clear, slow.

This is the case for a couple of hundred metres until a bridge, a rickety metal bridge. To be looked at, stepped on (no more than one at a time by the feel of it) but not crossed as it leads to the other side (#9).

Now onwards. A tiny wooden bridge – just a couple of planks with a metal handrail, takes us across a nameless tributary or field ditch, with another flat metal bridge to the left offering a further, to be spurned, chance of crossing the border (in any case this has a sign telling us to keep to the footpath).

Not long after this is a larger field gate to the left. Here we deviate from the river as it wends its way north then northeast, we will see it again soon enough. We carry straight on, keeping the band of trees to our left.

Soon a collapsing stile, which boasts "Works carried out by Dedham Vale and Stour Valley Project" with a phone number beginning 0473, the old code for Ipswich which changed in 1995! This must be from when the path first opened just the year before.

Still the band of trees to the left and the wheat field to our right. Now the band of trees thickens and the path disappears in to it, another collapsing stile, ivy coats the floor and myriad splinter branches weave their cobwebs over the under-storey.

To the left of another SVP waymarker, a tiny wooden footbridge takes us over another drainage ditch and through a kissing gate we are out in the open (#10).

At the time of writing the first thing to mention is a mobile field shelter. The path now goes down a grassy ride 20 metres wide between two groups of trees and soon follows the river again, just feet away, flat and placid, reedy, lilly-pad-covered, lovely. The cows to the right show little interest, which is fortunate. Any buildings to the left are those of Stoke College across the water.

At some points the river is uber-accessible, shallow beaches almost bidding you to walk in.

This all comes to an end as the flat concrete pads of the Stoke College Mill Gate Bridge are reached (#11). This takes its name from Stoke College just to the north, this was a college for priests dating back to 1415 and revived as an independent school in the 1950s. The place has associations with the de Clare family and a certain Mr Elwes, about whom more below.

This mill and mill-pond are part of the Stour water course and, quite unwittingly, that bridge has taken us in to Suffolk.

Beyond this, a last walk in the grass and a field gate with a kissing gate to its left. A short track of twenty metres and another side gate (all the time emblazoned with the SVP yellow arrow) and the muddy path takes us to the road. Ashen Lane.

Day One Part Three

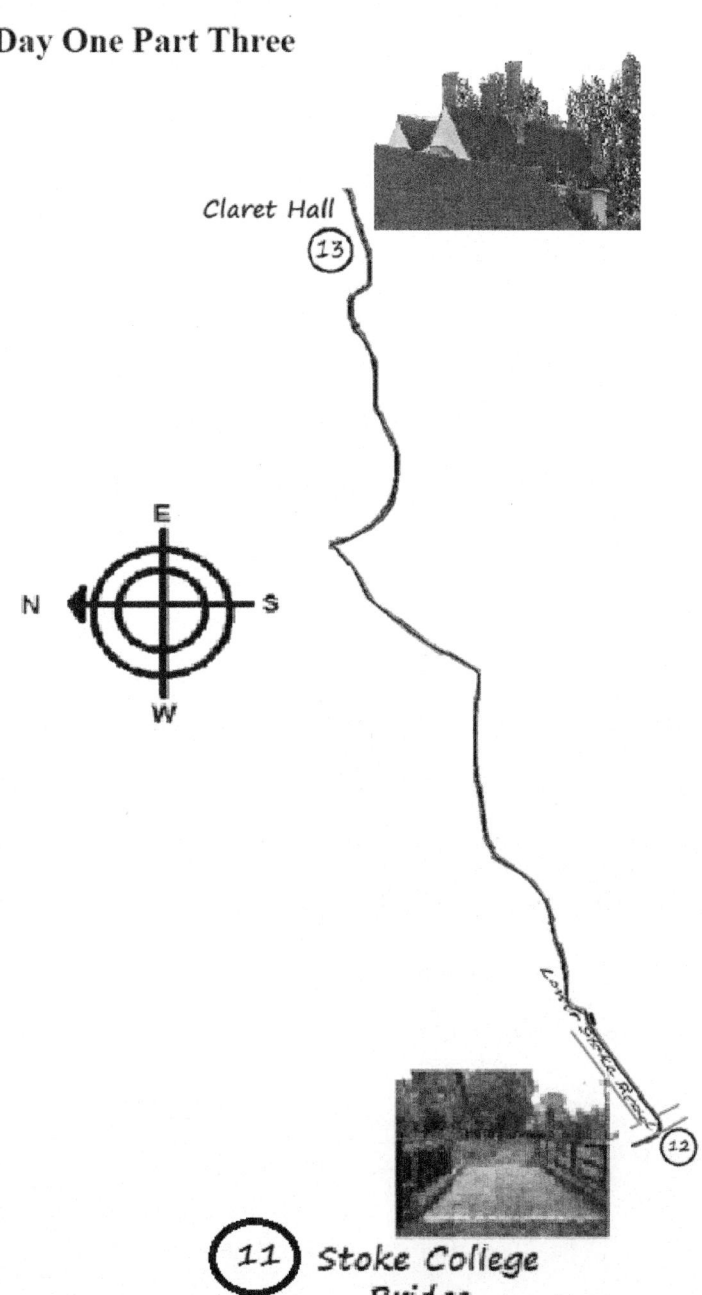

Claret Hall

(13)

Long Stoke Road

(12)

(11) Stoke College Bridge

Now is the crossroads of our choice. A left-hand turn will, in about half a mile, get us to Stoke-by-Clare, a comely place if with limited facilities. If the rules are to be broken, then Clare itself has much more to offer, so let's get back to the Essex-side, having been in Suffolk for 80 metres.

Turn right and down Ashen Lane, mostly road walking, but very quiet, in about 100 metres the white railings of a bridge appear and the Stour is re-crossed (#12).

Just ahead is a finger post, telling us that Ashen is to our right, Clare to our left. The latter is seawards, so there we go. Ashen, by the way, is a quiet little village with a mix of old and new properties and a population of about 300, sadly though it's about ¼ mile in the wrong direction.

This, the Lower Stoke Road, is mainly thin verge walking and is not the most thrilling part of the journey. It follows the Stour (with 100 metres of woodland in between) for about 100 metres before river and road go their own way at a point near Doctor's Lane (one of those little grassy triangular junctions), just past the Hadleigh Fishing Club sign (that's a highlight).

The road is straight, the odd passing place, overhanging oaks and nary a building until the cream farmhouse and black weather-boarded barns of a place called "Stours."

The land is rising gently, not a good sign if a river is being followed to the sea!

About 1.2km from the time we joined the road is a T-junction with a sign over to the right saying "Hollow Road", we go left.

Left here for Ashen Road

This is the Ashen Road (leading us away from that village we were near a little earlier), with more in the way of narrow verge walking and the road kinking around slightly rightwards, pass a gravelly path on the left and shortly (65 metres) past that is a footpath on the right. There are two choices here, carry on the road or cut across on the footpath. The point in common is the corner of Ashen Road and Bradley Hill. The former option is about 1km, the latter adds 500 metres (and still leaves you with 500 metres of verge walking). But it is generally not road-based and is worth the slight addition.

The footpath veers south briefly (150 metres), before checking back east through woodland for 150 metres, then with trees to the left and field to the right. It then re-enters woodland, shifting right (south-eastwards) for another 100 metres or so before breaking out in to the open. Here is why it is worth coming this way, at least for the setting and the story, if not for the fleeting glimpse, for here is Claret Hall (#13), another of the embarrassment of riches this part of the world has to offer in the way of country houses.

Right at the post for Claret Hall

Prog-rock band "The Enid" (no, I haven't heard of them either) and more famously Kim Wilde used the recording studio here. Further back (even than the 1980s) this was the pile of one John Elwes, MP, reputably the model for Dickens' scrooge (if the "M" stands for miserable, one shudders to think what the "P" stood for!).

Even further back, apparently Edward III's son Lionel lived here! Incidentally, this magnificent house was part of the Manor of Ashen, Ovington and Stoke-by-Clare, a sprawling landholding which covered both counties. Unfortunately, it is shrouded in walls, outbuildings and "keep out" signs, so you can't really have that good a look at it.

Claret Hall

Day One Part Four

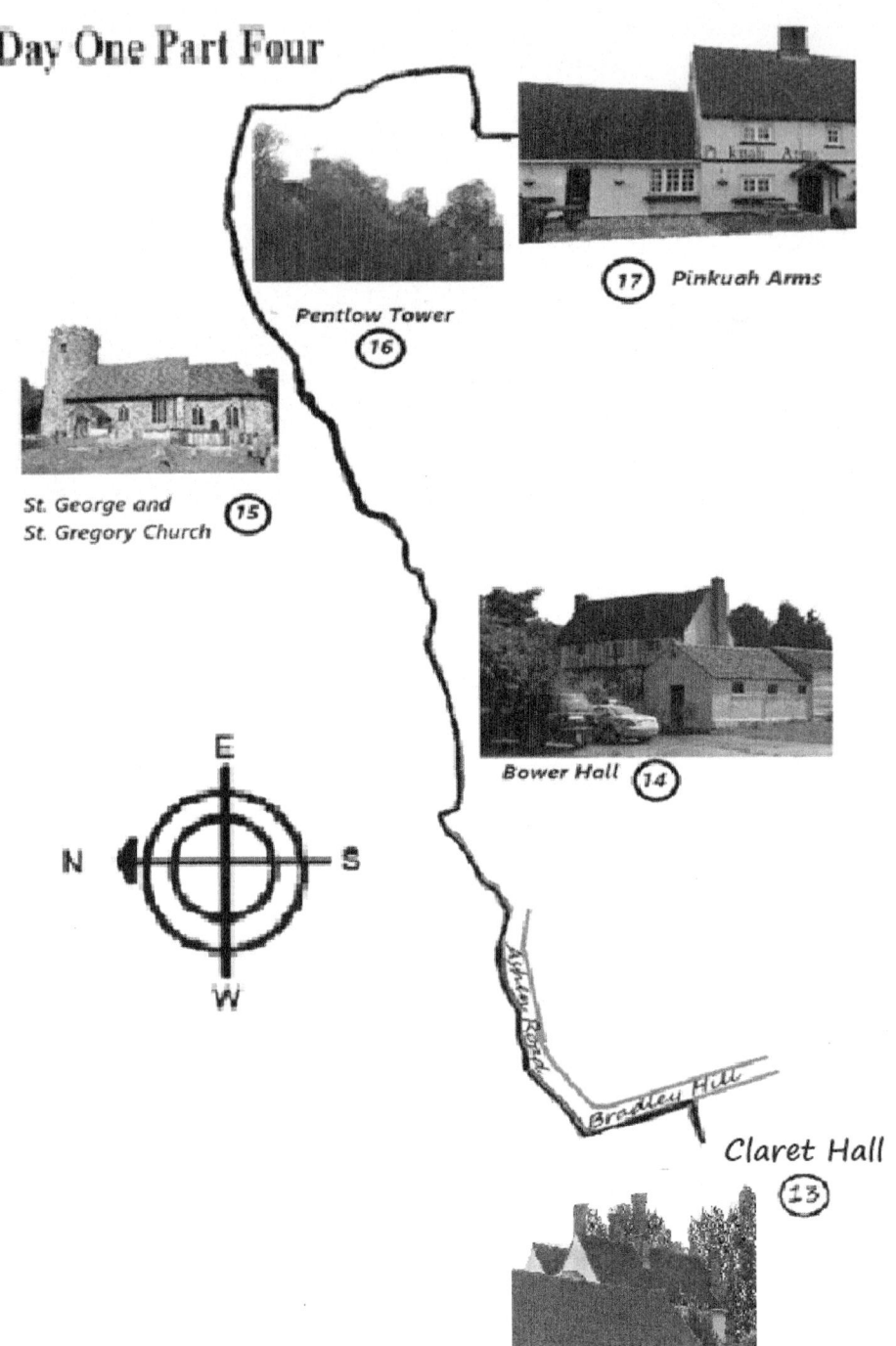

Pentlow Tower
(16)

(17) Pinkuah Arms

St. George and
St. Gregory Church (15)

Bower Hall (14)

Arlen Road

Bradley Hill

Claret Hall
(13)

200 metres past the building and the long straight drive comes to an end and a brick pillar bears the name of the place and it is time to leave.

A swift left on to Bradley Hill, with a gentle descent (riverwards) on a thin verge until 400 metres later is the aforementioned point in common.

The sign over the road tells us that Ashen is two miles to the left, and Clare one to the right. The houses in front are effectively a part of Clare, but are in Essex.

We have now been walking for about five miles. Not really a whole day's walk. Clare is a nice place, with more in it than its Stokey neighbour, tempting.

A hardened footway, lovely Rose Cottage. More, newer (1930s!) housing. 500 metres along, the houses peter out, 150 metres to a junction, rightwards signed towards Pentlow and the Belchamps, (or back to Ashen, or Ridgewell) hedges to chin height, pastoral views afar.

If opting for the shorter walk, Clare is the logical place to choose, not quite half way, but near enough and certainly worthy of a couple of hours' diversion at least (and perhaps overnighting) so carrying on would take us there – if not going all the way there, 400 metres along is Clare Priory which is just before the main river. This begs the question – was it once in Essex? A smaller strand of the Stour runs just to the south of the priory, however, and it may have been diverted at some point to create the watercourse we see today. In any event, this Franciscan priory is a quiet retreat and not necessarily for strolling around in.

Even if not going to Clare, the place is well worth a mention. Clare and all its lands once belonged to a Saxon thane called Aelfric, who gave them to St. John. However, after 1066 (and all that) it was all given to one of William's closest chums, one Richard fitz Gilbert of Bienfaite, Count of Brionne. This fiefdom included 170 manors, many in Suffolk. When Richard chose Clare as his HQ, he changed his name to Richard de Clare and a dynasty was born.

What's the relevance of this to Essex? Well, quite simply, given that only a narrow spit of water separated the two counties then as now, many of the lands owned by the de Clare tribe were in northern Essex and the de Clares lorded it over this part of the world for a long time. The history of Clare and Essex are thus entwined.

Enough of that though.

If the heroes' mile is sought however (especially if your car is in Sudbury/you're getting the train from there/that's where your B&B is!) we must turn right.

Following the same road along for about 800 metres, with the occasional magnificent pastoral views breaking out, the odd passing place is the only visual relent to a green corridor of soporific loveliness. Then is a gravelly path on the right, with a footpath sign hiding in the undergrowth, taking us to Cutbush Farm and nowhere else a mile and a half away.

Instead walk on and 250 metres more there is a concrete fingerpost to the left, the maps show this as going all the way to the river for a sniff of our lovely watercourse, but then to nowhere else.

This is Hickford Hill. Stick with the path another 100 metres and on the right "civilisation" shows itself briefly. A mown lawn and long driveway lead to yet another magnificent country farm house. This, though you cannot see it, is Claredown Farm where "g2 Energy completed the full Contestable and Balance of Plant design and build works on this 20MW, 33kV Battery Storage site in Essex." Apparently.

Just fifty metres more and a real footpath appears on the left, finger sign and all. This is not the SVP, that's the other side of the river at this point, but we have a real chance to get back to the object of our desire. At the time of writing a sign was in place, which whilst not appearing temporary, certainly was less permanent than the finger post, bearing the name "Rat's Castle."

Unabashed and jinking a little to the right, then left, this tree-lined path takes us to a place 400 metres along where the lily-pads can be almost heard, but then the river cruelly shies northwards and away from us.

No worries, 150 metres on we find it again or it us as it decides to loop back southwards and say hello. The Stour, for the first time since Stoke College Mill.

Cruelly, though, this is fleeting (50 metres maximum). Whilst the next 300 metres or so are glorious Stour-side right of way, they are also a dead-end.

To be enjoyed if you wish, but you will need to double-back. If the latter option has not been entertained, hang a right for 100 metres or so, then left, eastwards for about one kilometre.

Up Here, Then Left at the Hedge!

This crosses two fields, into a third:

Towards this copse

The tree cover thickens a little, a wide path is between two hedgerows, undulating towards a distant copse. When that copse is reached, there appear to be paths to the left and right of it, both going the same direction. Do not take the left path, it offers a couple of hundred metres of hope before running out into a tangled briar. So, with the copse to your left, proceed and this eventually cuts a thin path between the trees. There are glimpses of the gurgling river through gaps between the trees over left.

As we break cover, there is a pumping station in all its brick-built glory, then a flat concrete bridge to Suffolk at Cherry Tree Barn. A sign tells us that we are the Bower Hall Bore Hole.

A mansard roofed red brick building over left and the footpath becomes a track, becomes a lane, becomes a road. A steep-sided barn conversion is on our right.

Another 200 metres along, the clutter of farm buildings leads us to Bower Hall, Pentlow (#14); a predictably fine 1600's yellow timber-framed lovely.

With that on your right, the peaceful river appears on your left. All is most tranquil and pleasant and it would be tempting to linger, but it does feel private and carry on we must, armed only with a photographic snippet of what is for them their every day.

A little bit of paradise

Right around the building and up the grassy ride, a paddock on the left with fluttering stake and rope demarking it. Past a small wooden stable building and left around the big tree.

Follow the meandering field edge path, towering trees to the north blocking views of our Stour but doing nothing to shade us from the sun. 1,500 metres on, it disappears in to the woods, branches bowing overhead. 100 metres or so and the path breaks out again into the open, with clear views to the north in the gap between the groups of trees.

Heading rightish (north-eastwards), with the trees on your left, 600 metres elapse and the stepped brick wall and buildings of the grey-gault Georgian Pentlow House and its neighbours can be seen.

As the path meanders rightwards away from this group of buildings, a pair of Essex pigs (the ones with the thick black band) are sizzling in the sun. A sign on the gate advises us that "Chicken George's Eggs" are "For Sale at the Front Gate" eggs and bacon – all in one place!

Egg and bacon anyone?

Meanwhile another sign advises us that the fence is electric – there's the cooking sorted out!

Emerging on to the Pentlow Road, a finger post straight ahead points to Pentlow and The Belchamps on the right, behind to Cavendish and Clare and ahead to Foxearth and Sudbury.

The latter is nearest to (although not near enough) the Stour and potentially very long, without much visual relief or any chance of a drink (or anything else). But we take it, for now.

But first, having crossed the road, and taken the thin path rightwards, you will pass a cream rendered property, and in the background may spot something rather wonderful, some crenulations atop a small tower.

Immediately past that property, before a paddock, is a thin stony track with a parish noticeboard. This leads to the lovely St. George and St. Gregory Church (#15) with a splendid round bell tower. This building is Saxon in origin, dating from 650-850. It is one of only four round towered churches in Essex, the tower dating from about 1320.

Inspired, if you'll pardon the pun, carry on for 500 metres, with verge-ways spanning from expansive to negligible. A couple of hundred metres in, there are farm buildings on the right and the verge reaches its most generous proportions.

A hundred or so metres more and just as things have got to their narrowest, the road bends away left and just before the trees end is an opening on the right. This is Hoe Lane.

And here is a point where choices need to be made....

Hoe Lane, where choices are to be made....

To be faithful to an as near as possible river walk, one should carry on along the verge-way, bending right then left, into Pentlow Street, touching the river, then the man -made lakes of the Foxearth Fisheries and the Foxearth Nature Reserve, perhaps catching distant views across the Stour of Philips Avent (where they make those baby milk bottles). Then turning south and eventually finding Liston and its lovely church and hall, before finally reaching Rodbridge Corner.

Pleasant enough, but three-and-a-half miles for a fairly limited return – and no chance of a pub or even light refreshment on the way.

Or....

You can shave half a mile off and go to a pub, possibly. Yes, a pub, hopefully (the venue in question has lurched from opening to closure in recent times). And there's a folly on the way and the rather lovely village of Foxearth.

So, Hoe Lane it is. The lane is marked by a wooden fingerpost, and a new sign informing you that cars (and indeed horses and carts!) shall not pass between 1st November and 31st March. this will take us to the village of Pentlow proper and to two points of potential interest. It also shaves off a bit in the corner which does not have much interest (and from which the river cannot be easily seen for the most part).

About 300 metres down, a path veers off to the right, hugging lagoons and farm buildings. Here is School Barn Farm. 400 metres more and you may catch glimpses, amongst the trees, of an uncharacteristically large edifice. This is Pentlow Tower (#16), a Victorian curio also known as Bull's Folly. The 95ft tower was erected in 1859 by the Rev. Edward Bull, in memory of his parents Rev John and Mrs Margaret Bull "on a spot that they loved so well." It is not publicly accessible (being in a private garden) and comprises a spiral staircase of 114 steps. The detailing of contrasting bricks is a visual delight and redolent of the Jacobean style of Layer Marney Tower some way to the south of Colchester.

The house itself "Pentlow Tower, Pentlow, Suffolk"....hold on a minute, where? Is described on Historic England's website as being from c1880 and built for Reverend *John* Bull – some possible confusion there. It is a wedding venue, open for hire, but not accessible otherwise. It also offers a series of "Mindfulness" sessions etc.

Onto the main road and the "it's not quite as far as the other way" bonus is almost cancelled out as we turn right, past a red telephone box, and soon left down the sleepy and be-bungalowed Pinkuah Lane and 100 metres down is the Pinkuah Arms (#17). Sadly, currently, shut.

Still the pub experience alludes us.

If you're wondering about the unusual name, Pinkuah is actually pronounced "Pink H'us". It is a corruption of the name of the house 'The Pink House'. Legend (and various Google searches) has it that the landlord, some time ago, tired of it being called merely the "Pink H'us", and grandified it as 'The Pinkuah Arms' so he could display a second-hand pub-sign of a coat of arms that he had bought in a junk shop.

He even invented a former lord of the manor to whom he attributed this heraldry, but nobody could ever trace such a person.

The modified word, though, has given its name to the little lane.

Day One Part Five

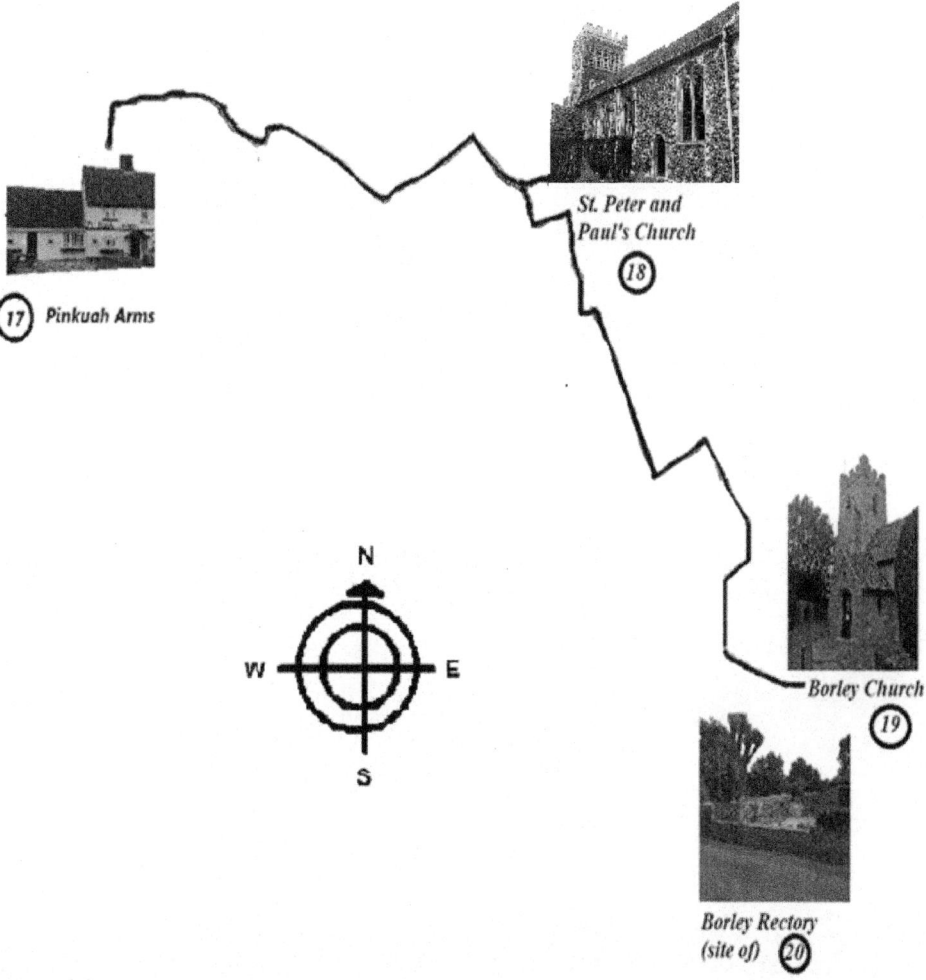

St. Peter and Paul's Church (18)

Pinkuah Arms (17)

Borley Church (19)

Borley Rectory (site of) (20)

After that, back up Pinkuah Lane and right, 700 metres and the road bends right (there is enough verge to help) low industrial buildings appear on the left, "Daniel Piper Motor Services" a grassy triangle, turn left, a lime-rendered house on the left, then just beyond and opposite is a footpath right, take this for 150 metres then just past a ménage (right) is a divergence of paths, take the RHS one. This for 400 metres.

Left here

On your right is a charming white thatched house. Turn left, on to a narrow road for 400 metres, a paddock to your right, soft but narrow verges on either side.

As this reaches a main road, on the left is a road sign pointing back to The Belchamps, left to Pentlow, Cavendish and Clare and right to Long Melford and Sudbury. It is the latter we turn to. Just over the road are the sweet white buildings of Foxearth Hall Barns. Charming, sixteenth century building, wedding venue. Foxearth Hall itself is a II* listed building and has parts dating back to the 13th century.

A moat to your left, carry on, newer houses, a long high cob wall on the left, thatched cottages, the cob drops down to a metre-high red brick affair with a hedge on. Where there is a break in this (not the little one at Cook's Cottage, the next one) a 100-odd metre walk down a little lane will take you to St. Peter and Paul's Church (#18) - making up for Liston. There has been a church here since the 13th century the pretty crenellated church tower looks oddly-truncated. That is because the spire (130 feet high) was lost in a storm in 1948.

The interior of the church does contain some lovely touches, including wall paintings of the type that the Reformation put paid to. These seem to have survived all that madness.

Emerging and left down the street, the cob has emerged in dwarf form. Eventually, with some exquisite alms houses on the right, the vista opens up and the main centre of Foxearth (such as it is) is here, with its charming village sign. Now we are about three miles from the end of the walk.

The village hall is straight ahead, turn left.......there on the left is a beautiful old school and the cob is in full height and charming rendered houses are on the right, left is Foxearth House.

As the village begins to runs out we turn right down Claypits (sign-posted Claypit Hall, Brook Hall Only) for 150-odd metres are houses left and right, these then disappear and the road narrows, with just hedges on both sides, 150 metres more and the road forks by a stand of trees – take the left turn just by sign telling you "Brook Hall Only."

This stretch is only for about 30 metres, then is a quick right across the field. This footpath goes for 1 kilometre due south-southeast, more or less in a straight line (although some maps show a bit of a "kink" leftwards after about 100 metres.

After the first field, the path crosses a pasture for about 150 metres (bisected by a hedge), then back in to an open field for another 250 metres before it hits a hedgerow and sends you leftwards. When this emerges on to a dusty (or muddy) path by a fingerpost, turn right and head south, past a rambling pink pile, down a narrow lane (with a ditch to your left) until 250 metres since first you hit the road, a grassy triangle.

On this is a finger post, showing "Borley Green Only" in one direction, The Belchamps and Bulmer in another and "Borley, Foxearth, Long Melford" in the other. This is counter-intuitive as we've just *been* to Foxearth and are going *to* Borley. However, don't forget that these signs are for motorists, and the direct route we've just taken twixt one and t'other is verboten to the iron horse.

So left it is, along Hall Road (incidentally, an overnight option could be the Borleymere Shepherd's Hut "Luxury Glamping in Suffolk", ok, we'll let that one go – it's about 500 metres in the other direction) and within 200 metres we are in Borley.

Already, between the squat red brick houses, the church tower can be seen over-left. Eventually the white-rendered farmhouse and its cob wall and moat, followed by a polite Georgian specimen set back, then a twisted barn conversion and, 200 metres from the beginning of the village, there is the little churchyard and, beyond this, the church (#19).

No ghost-hunters please!

Borley Church dates from several ages, its knave potentially being late-Saxon or very early Norman, much of it being medieval, it is Grade I listed. This and Foxearth have far outweighed Liston, but there is more to come.

Cross the road, this is Borley! Everyone has heard of Borley Rectory (#20), surely? This, by reputation, is (was) the site of the "most haunted" place in Britain. Was, because it burnt down in 1939.

Rife are the tales of the ghost of a nun, of a phantom coach ridden by headless horsemen. No way to prove this of course. What could be proven was the skull of a young woman found in a brown paper bag in 1927 and the bones of a young woman found in the cellar after the fire. All-in-all, just a bit too creepy!

Turning left out of the churchyard, the site of the rectory is almost opposite, behind a cob wall and the entrance drive to "The Old Coach House."

There is nothing obviously left of the old place, except perhaps the odd tormented soul (still looking for a pub that's open).

The site of Borley Rectory

Day One Part Six

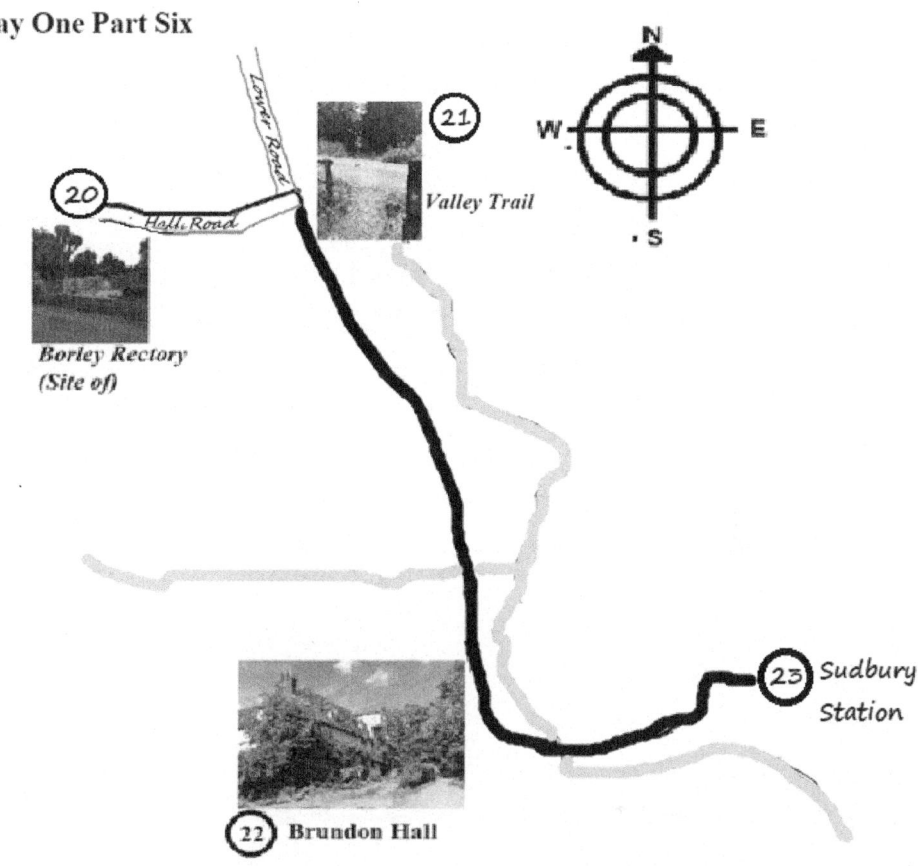

With that on your right, carry on and save half a kilometre by not re-joining the footpath which takes you north-east, instead carry on down Hall Road and use the thin verges and driveway accesses where possible, passing a couple of houses on the right early on, before a long walk to the next pair of semis and the beautifully delicate Borley Village Hall on the left.

Hall Road now runs out as a vastly over-extended pair of semis crashes in to view from the left.

On the right is a smaller road and just yards later, behind some small collapsible bollards, is "The Valley Trail" (#21) from "Suffolk County Council" – now hold on a minute! We haven't crossed the Stour, so how is that so?

Right here for the Stour Valley Trail

Well, this neck of the woods had the flag of the three swords flying over it, first as a kingdom and later as a county, throughout all of its history until 1888, and all because of pooh. Yes pooh.

Sanitary districts were introduced to England in 1973 and 1875. Ballingdon found itself in the same district as nearby (but over the river) Sudbury. The Local Government Act of 1888 sought to rationalise all of this. With a number of urban sanitary districts laying in more than one county, the boundaries were altered so that each town was completely within the administrative county containing the largest part of the district's population. So it was that lovely Ballingdon, which we shall see shortly, and all its surroundings (including Brundon) lay down their three swords and instead picked up, well, a sort of ship on top of some strange flag things and two crowns and a sun, or whatever all that is on Suffolk's coat of arms.

And this wasn't the only area where this happened. Remember that first day? Land to the south of the Stour where the land is administered by the other side? Parts of Haverhill and Kedington were also transferred then. If they hadn't been, the walk on the first day would have been a couple of miles longer, so not all bad then.

This winding path, well, winds and wends its way for a mile-and-a-half southwards, between two lines of trees.

There is a point where one can deviate from this, adding scarcely a few metres to the journey.

Just after a flat, metal-edged bridge crossing Belchamps Brook (below), a divergence of paths shows itself about a sign for the Valley Trail with a map of the Gainsborough Trail (so many trails) on it. Taking the left fork, the following views are more interesting than the endless sylvan tunnel (which of itself is not unpleasant).

The narrow track leads to soft meadows grazed by beautiful horses and soon a field gate (which has an easy space to the left towards a group of buildings.

Whilst there is a pleasant enough grey-rendered house straight ahead, it is the buildings over left (and constituting a very slight detour) which are of note – and definitely worth the detour of little over fifty metres.

Here is the charming Brundon Mill (#22) and its associated cottages, all in pink render and boarding. Nearby amongst the trees is Brundon Hall.

Back to the path (called Brundon Lane at this point) and left for about 500 metres before the path re-joins the Stour Valley Path, straight as a die heading south, past the AFC Sudbury football ground (I wonder if they know they're really in Essex), then crossing over the A131, with views of pretty Ballingdon (in historic Essex) to the left and right.

Ballingdon is an oddity, not just because it is really in Essex, but because it appears disproportionately grand for what is, according to the maps at least, just a suburb of Sudbury.

There is, of course, a reason for this. Before the transfer to Suffolk, it was cheaper to open a business on the Essex side of the river, as no levy was due to Sudbury town council. This meant that Ballingdon became the business district of Sudbury.

So much for history.

All this side of the little bridge used to be in Essex

And all of this too!

What you do now depends on where you intend to sleep tonight. As you arrive in Ballingdon, the footpath passes over the A131, peel off right and it will take you on to that same road. At the bottom turn right and admire the faded charm of those old buildings (remembering that, for all but the last 100 years, these were in Essex) and about 50 yards down on the left-hand side is "Genesis" – a place to stay. Also in Ballingdon is Ballingdon Mill 200 metres further along. If not that, then a further 100 metres along and in Suffolk proper is the Riverside Bar (which has rooms?)

If none of that is for you, then press on.

Eventually (300 metres after the A131) the path takes us across a muddy bridge, across the Stour to Suffolk, *real* Suffolk – always been Suffolk Suffolk – not a bit it nicked off Essex. (from here, the walk will be reversed for the Sudbury – Nayland stretch tomorrow).

The bridge to proper Suffolk

300 metres along the wooded path, we cross a tributary, shown on the maps (imaginatively) as "The River Stour." 300 metres more and we break out in to the car park at Waitrose. You are there, you are in Sudbury, the first day's walk is all but done. Now it's just a question of where to finish off. If the car is to be retrieved, then retrieve it; if the hotel beckons it is only a stone's throw away with a well-deserved shower and meal not far off, or if the train is your vehicle of choice then the station (#23) is just a few hundred metres around to your right.

That is day one completed and a lot of ground covered. Time to reflect on a magical day in the unknown fields of north Essex, with so much more to come.

Day Two – From Sudbury to Nayland (12 miles)

Two-day short walk option, staying in Bures (Essex/Suffolk)

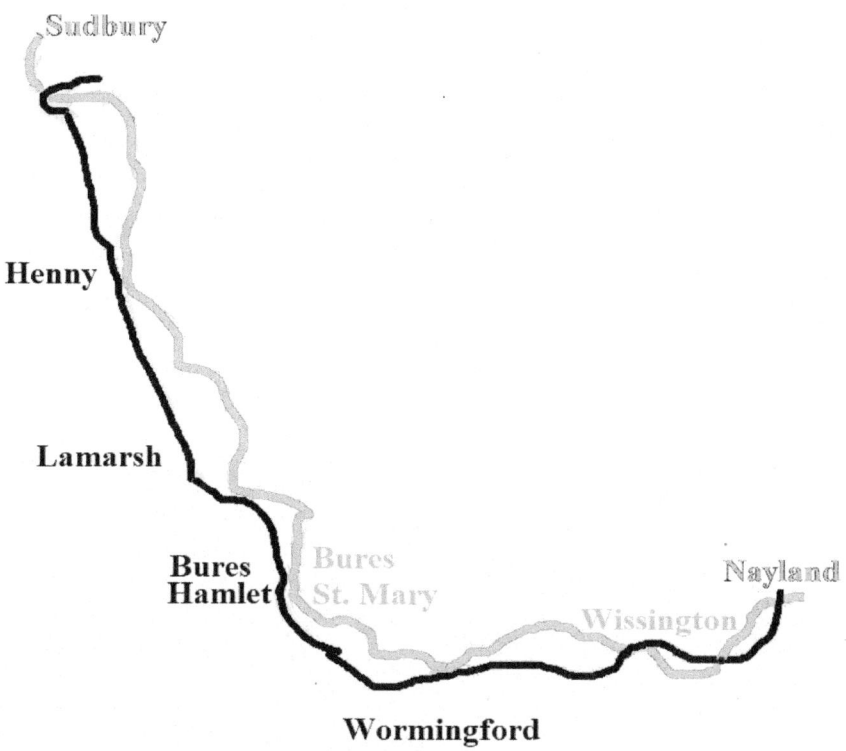

In many ways Day Two is more straightforward than yesterday. The walk is largely on footpaths (although there is some road and verge walking) and is, by and large, closer to the Stour. The scenery ranges from comparatively lofty heights to lowland pasture and, at Wormingford, we officially arrive in Constable Country – Dedham Vale.

Day Two Part One

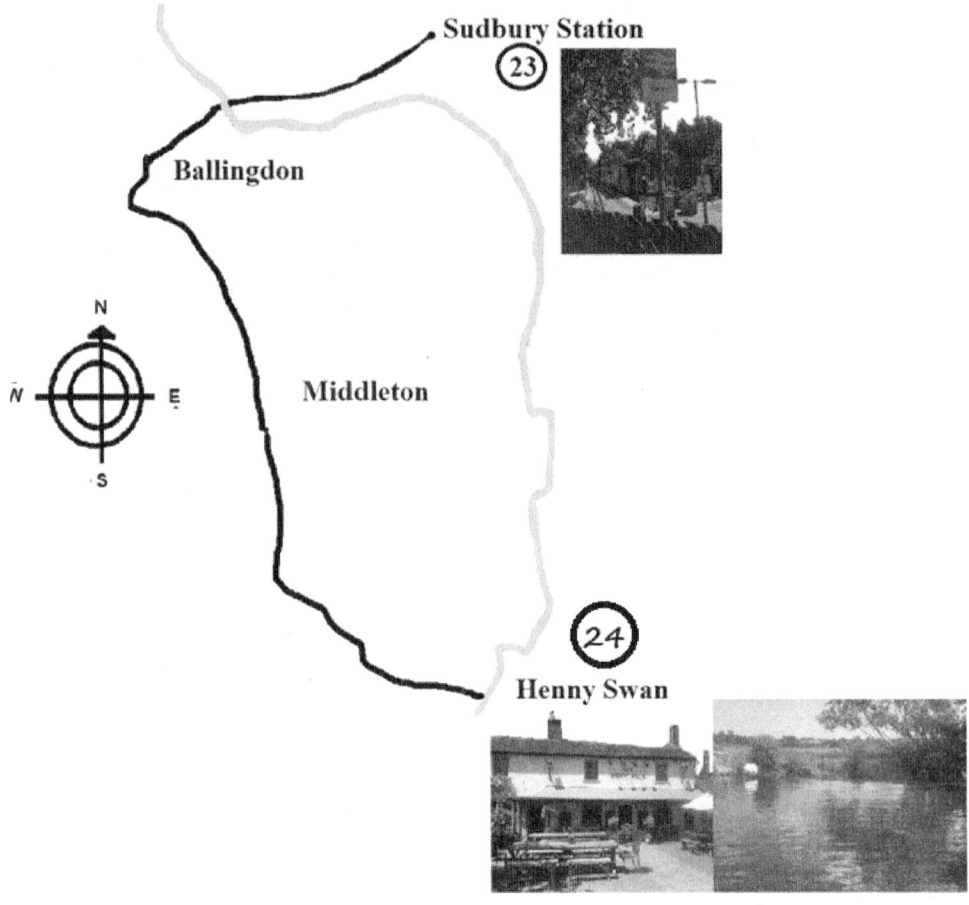

The proximity to Sudbury station means that, if a short walk is desired after yesterday's marathon (well, half marathon strictly speaking) then some judicious use of car and train can be employed by parking up at Bures, taking the hourly train service (a seven -minute journey) and walking back to your car.

This trick can also be used later on in the journey, but enough of that. Let's kick off.

We are in Suffolk and, as taken from the "Waitrose turning" the first kilometre is a reverse of yesterday. Along The Valley Trail, the river on our left still (but we are walking inland briefly) over that little tributary and then until that muddy bridge. Now left and over the glassy Stour into old Essex.

Just short of Ballingdon, a path peels away downwards to the left. Take this (or some steps a bit later, it makes no difference) and soon at the bottom you will see a sign for Kone Vale a "Local Wetland and Woodland Site" boasting the Speckled Wood Butterfly and all other forms of obscura.

Turn left and follow the mud path through the grass for about 250 metres, trees either side, as mid-20th century housing heaves in to view. Between the pink rendered end terrace house and the field gate advance on to Middleton Road and briefly left, then crossing over and up Meadow View Road. This curls around left until the grassy spaces of Pinecroft Rise can be seen and we turn right. With a thin stand of trees on your left, two-thirds of the way up the green space you will see a finger sign pointing off leftish. This arrows us to a dog bin and, more importantly, the Stour Valley Path and a gap between a house and some grassy tussocks.

The next 300 metres are woodland, edging ever upwards and soon giving us surprisingly elevated views between the trees over Sudbury and the surrounding area.

The path, having taken a fairly consistent southerly route since entering the woods, now breaks out into the open by a further SVG sign and the rolling arable outlook is most, most pleasant.

The direction is the same for the next 800 metres, passing close by (and largely from view) Middleton Garage Services and other automobile concerns after the first 100 metres. A further 300-odd metres you are near the small village of Middleton, also left. There is a quaint old church, with a 12th century knave and medieval additions, but this can only be accessed via a one-kilometre detour. If you have that in you, take the path left which begins at a junction of routes after you've passed Middleton and heads back where you've come from, then follow the very narrow "The Street" then Rectory Road all the way around to the left. This is quite a detour for another, albeit exquisite, little church.

Instead, push on south. About 350 metres more, a path deviates off on the left from the SVG (and, indeed, St. Edmunds Way, as it is at this point). This is just after a small copse on your left and as views break out between this and a band of trees to your right. It is tempting to take it, but it just arches back near to Middleton as well (that's a lot of footpaths for a little place!), so press on!

Trees to your right, into the next field, 200 metres more and there is a charming spot to sit. A large tree and a slate bench remembering Amanda MacDonald who died tragically young (1957-2001) who lived in Little Henny "My little bit of heaven." A lovely place to stop and ponder a moment.

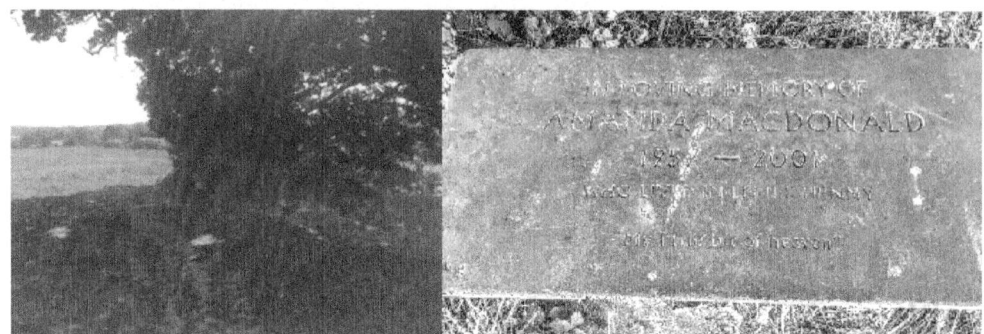

150 metres more, and time for a change as we look for Amanda's Little Henny and a spot of lunch. Where a much-badged wooden stake shows us the different paths, we go left.

This path hugs the odd-shaped field edges, meaning the 1 kilometre to our pub is for the crows. The first bit is open, straight on, then sweeping around to the left. As this enters the next field, go right for 250 metres, then disappearing between trees and a tiny footbridge crosses an almost not there stream.

There are options here, but the easiest to recount is a swift right near said bridge, for 100 metres and then the path hits a road. The signpost carries the footpath on, but you must head left. Some field-edge walking is necessary on the left. An act of slight trespass means that you can walk inside the hedge for the last 250 metres and emerge unscathed on to Henny Road at the time of writing.

The next bit is a detour of 300 metres, but so worth it. Turning left, pass a red telephone box, using whatever relief the odd driveway provides, a most magnificent country house with its cob walls on the left, then the amazing Henny Swan (#24).

Its garden spills over the road into lawns which roll down to the Stour where, as a bonus, boats arrive and leave for Sudbury, kayakers picking their way between.

Despite this, the Stour is at its most placid – glassy waters and pastoral views off of Constable's own easel.

If you have time, walk on 100 metres more in the wrong direction and, after some newer housing, enjoy on the left the gorgeous chocolate box white thatched cottages. However, the Henny Swan is enough to fill the heart, and sumptuous fayre the stomach.

Day Two Part Two

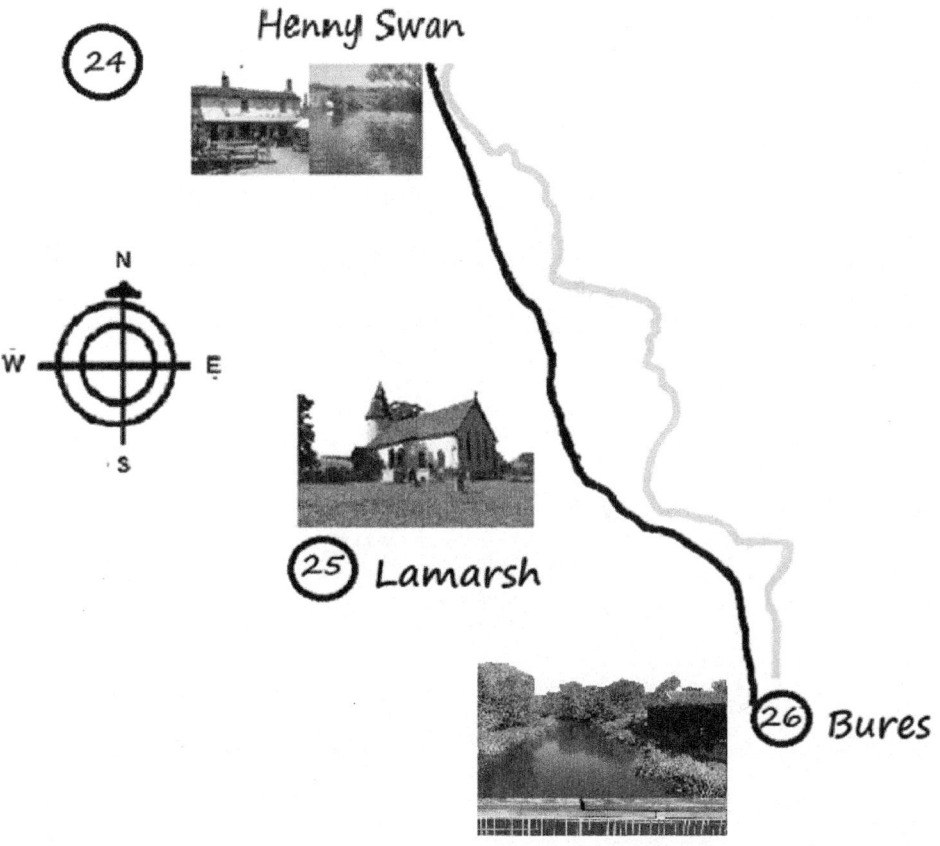

River on our left again, we push on past that cob wall and country house and pass the point at which we entered Henny Road a whole mealtime ago. Notice to the left a wooden footbridge crossing to the other place, but push on ahead.

A sign post offers us Sudbury, Great Henny and Lamarsh/Bures. It is the latter we seek.

Do not cross this little bridge!

We pass Lodge Cottage and Lower Farm Cottages and Snells Farmhouse and Old Fenners and some delightful but unidentified thatched cottages 150 metres on from the signpost. Then the harsher dwelling with gates and security intercom which speaks of the newcomer.

The rustic black barns of Boutells Farm on the right as the land dips down and we pass the sign for Lamarsh. There is generally room to be safe here, but the banks steepen at this point and the road climbs, tyre marks on the verges providing somewhere to walk. A parent and child road-sign indicates that road walking is *de rigeur* here as the odd driveway to the odd farm building acts as refuge to the almost non-existent traffic.

Another road sign, offering Sudbury, Bures or Twinstead. Well, we're technically in Lamarsh (#25), that's why that's off the sign – Bureswards it is.

Soon is Daws Hall on the left, a nature reserve. There inside, a blue plaque on a building commissioned by The Braintree Society, proudly boasts "Robert Bamford, Racing Cyclist, Motor Engineer and co-founder of Aston Martin" was born at Daws Hall on 16th June 1883. Well I never.

As we pass Pitmire Lane on the left, a beautiful, large white thatched Tudor cottage is on the right, with its range of buildings behind.

The next 500 metres are quiet, an area of rough grass on the right provides safe walking (or at least refuge, it is fairly steep) and views open up of the river valley; the Stour now half a mile away. In between, the two-carriage train picks its way through, shuttling between Sudbury and Bures.

As the trees close in on the left, they partly shroud a group of farm buildings, views of which now open up until the low-set brick and tile range hems the very road itself. This is Lamarsh Hall, stolen views of which are eventually gleaned through the trees. It is a magnificent building, Tudor with a jettied first floor and clay peg tiles.

Then, just beyond its lawns is an absolute gem (another one) Lamarsh Church of the Holy Innocents. White, round-towered and, of course, worth a peek inside.

This is another of the round-towered churches, dating from Norman to 14th century times, with a beginning date of probably 1140. This is Grade I listed. The spire was capped in this odd way in 1865. Inside clear to see are the barrel-roof rafters, stained glass windows etc.

Of particular note is the memorial plaque to the fallen of the Great War and a reminder that scarcely a single parish was left unscathed. Nine names are on display, but it is chilling to find that there are three sets of names repeated – the Baldwin, Buckingham and Hayward families lost two members each.

On a hot day, this cool building is a Godsend, but it gives us not our daily bread (or lemonade), for that we must move on.

Incidentally "Lamarsh" is not old French for "the marsh" as you may think (though there is marshland nearby), no it is more boring than that. Marsh means "stubble land" and lam = loam. There you have it, loamy stubble land. Probably the most celebrated local was Margaret Beaufort, mother of Henry VII (she was lady of the manor, but doesn't appear to have lived here).

Moving off from the church, the land is steeply-banked on the right, so no going there, it's back on the road. Soon the houses start to collect on the left, then the right. Then is the tiny village hall, left, which may have been a school. It has that 1890s red brick board school look to it.

The land on the left side of the road (still called Henny Road by the way) opens up left, whilst on the right 1960's bungalows are set back behind an impressively deep greensward.

After an impressively pargetted – garage (!) on the right, we pass Alphamstone Road (right) and 100 metres on the increasingly narrow road bends around left and finally we are free of Henny Road and on the Bell Hill as Hornes Green is signed on our right.

Now is a mown lawn on our right, which is separated from front gardens by a line of spindly trees. As we walk this and the road bends away rightwards, the cream-yellow gable end of a building opens up, soon revealing itself to be a pub!

This is the Lamarsh Lion which, like so many other rural hostelries, has had some hard times. However, it is alive and well and is run as a community pub.

Time to slake our first before the next part of the journey.

Job done, and Bures the next point of interest. We head off and about 75 metres along it's finally time to say goodbye to the road which has been with us for the two miles since the Henny Swan.

A finger post gives us Sudbury, Bures and "Private Road" the latter is unmade, lightly trafficked and is the official footpath, so we peel off to the left.

Another delightful country house, cream rendered and peg-tiled is soon on the right. Then left is Edgar's Farm and a honeycomb-coloured thatched cottage and we are spoilt by the bucolic perfection of it all.

Over-left is an elevated view of the railway line, which we will see soon enough.

400 metres since turning off from the road, we pass another exquisite pink pile on our right and disappear into the trees, emerging on to the line itself.

Just in here

A sign warns us not to trespass under pain of a £1000 fine; however, the stile makes it clear enough that this is the way we must go.

Go carefully. You would have to be bloody unlucky, statistically, to be hit by a train on this quiet branch line, but one unlucky mistake is all it requires.

Over the line, over the next stile, a fresh and grassy path awaits us.

In and about woodland for 100 metres and at last we are reunited once more with the reason for our journey. Kayakers can be seen, come down from the Henny Swan, young Friesians graze amongst the old man's beard and all the air is stiflingly late summer, good old gin and tonic weather.

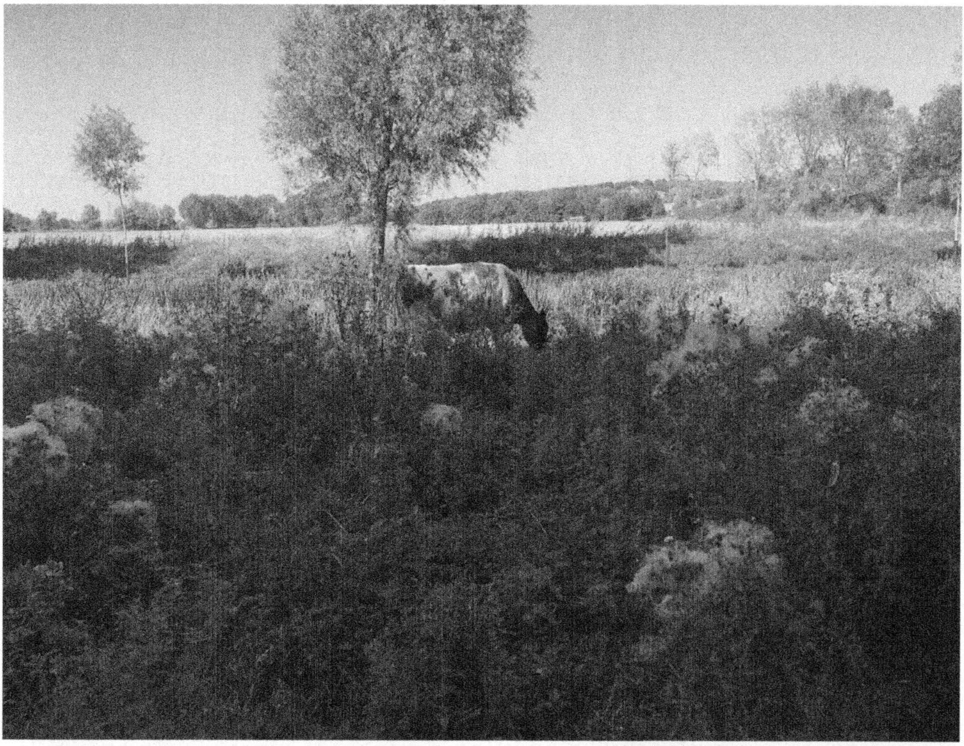

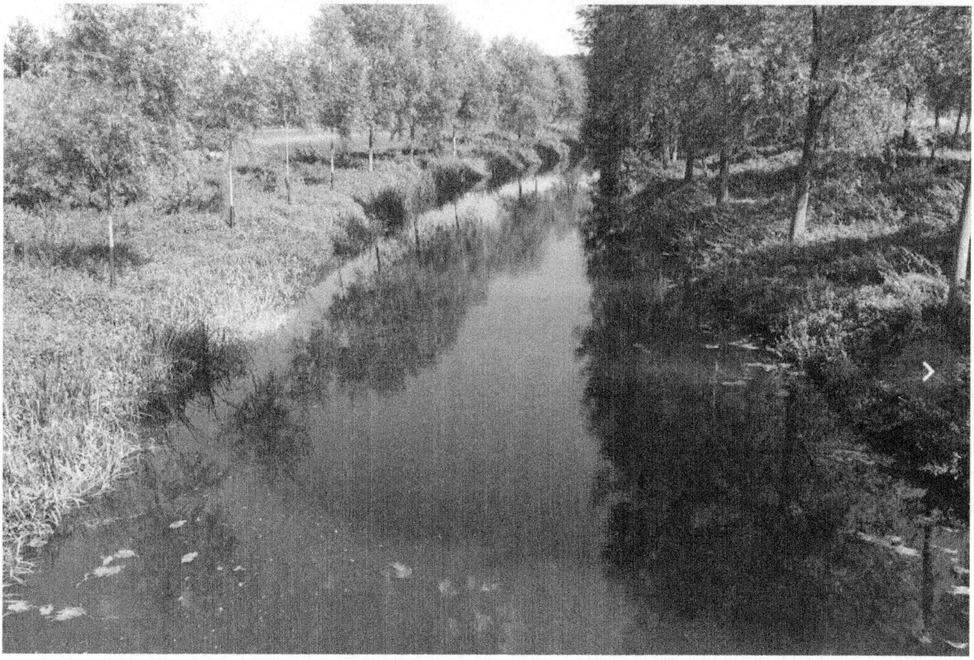

350 metres from the level crossing is a little bridge which allows us to stand and admire.

Breaking out between lines of trees and on to an agricultural field, we arrow rightwards and south-east away from the river, it being denied us by one field just 100 metres left, such are the laws of trespass.

The path kinks slightly more to the right and in a southerly direction as it enters another field (barely distinguished from its neighbour by rough grass and the odd tree), and carries on for 500 metres more, before a path appears on the left. This gives a quick and lovely view again, trees reflected, branches hanging.

Moving back to the main path and 200 metres along are the first signs of "civilisation" i.e. Bures.

Agricultural buildings right and works are being done to a fine old crumbling red brick wall. Pretty soon a wall on our right acts to create a corridor, the pink/orange-rendered building to our left adorning the other wall. This, it turns out, is a hairdresser's/beautician's as we emerge on to Station Hill.

Bures (#26). As to the what next, that depends on how you got here. If by car and you used the station, then that is (as the name suggests) just up the road (rightwards) about 200 metres. As for a B&B – well. The maps do not seem to suggest any such. However, further searches bring up the Rivendell Suite

Depending on how you are set up, you might have to take the train back to Sudbury, crazy as that might seem, (or to Marks Tey, but although that has a hotel it is not so near the station, and although adequate hardly fits with the bucolic escapism of this jaunt) or drive to a hotel in nearby villages such as Stoke-by-Nayland.

DAY TWO PART THREE

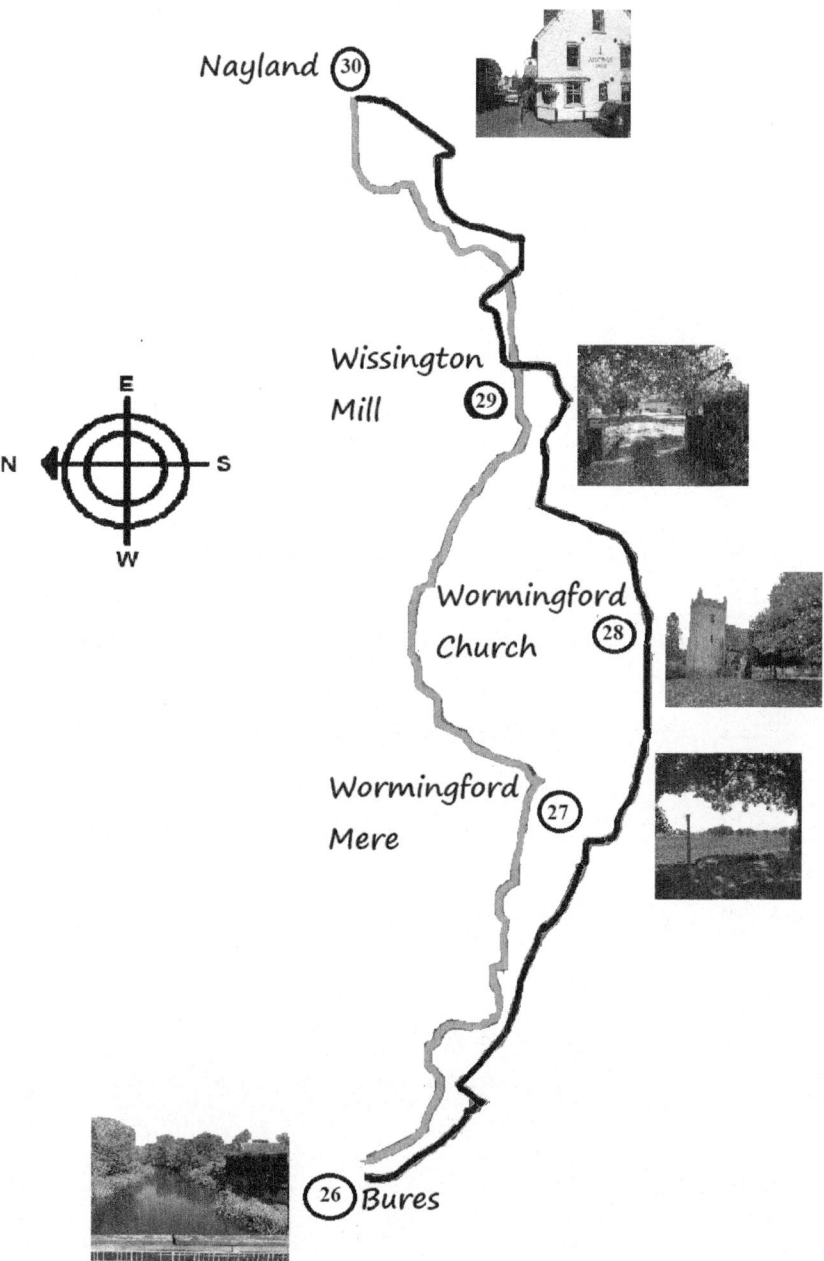

Nayland ㉚

Wissington Mill ㉙

Wormingford Church ㉘

Wormingford Mere ㉗

㉖ Bures

Or, if you are up for a long day – walk on. And if you want an even longer day, go to the pub – the Eight Bells is just opposite and 100 metres down the road.

You will have noted opposite and just before the pub, signage pointing you to Sudbury or Colchester. The latter is correct and this is Colchester Road. Note also the village sign for "Bures Hamlet" as the Essex side is known (and by some chance was never pilfered by Suffolk) and a further sign remembering good Queen Elizabeth's jubilee (the first one, that is the first jubilee).

We need to cross the road where safe to go back to the river side of things. A row of one and a half storey white cottages followed by a hand car wash give the impression of a mixed bag, but this soon gives way to a generally pleasant palette of residences. The river is glimpsed between buildings, with back gardens to envy: names like "Riverside" and "The Boat House" telling us what we already know.

A couple of hundred yards down, though, views do open up and just beyond this a footpath leads leftwards and to the river – DO NOT TAKE THIS! It leads to a lovely bridge and over, but takes us no further on this side.

Here is the bridge to wrongness

It is a bit of verge-side walking required for us (easily wide enough to be safe) for another 700 metres. The verge does narrow in places, but again has that "parent and child" warning triangle. A brick bridge spans a narrow stream (Cambridge Brook) half way and eventually, some form of man re-emerges, a garden fence and a road junction to the right and, on the left a footpath next to Brook House Cottage.

This disappears between the garden wall of the latter and field edge, trees to the left for 150 metres.

Then is a field gate to go over or around and the path kicks off to the right. A little while on, the merest of diversions left will offer views of the river, Bures Mill and the mill-pond on the Suffolk side.

We are now back on the Stour Valley Path. Heading right now, for about 500 metres (including a kissing gate), cuts out a meander and the path leads us south-eastwards towards and indeed to the river. Soon is another kissing-gate amongst the tanglewood and then next to a public footpath stake little more than a plank with a metal hand-rail over another tiny stream.

At a choice of paths choose the left-hand-side. Carry on in the same direction (eschewing any further leftward ambling as this will get you in to a pickle). 200 metres in front of you is a black weather-boarded farm building. On arriving, this turns out to be the fenced off "Wormingford Pumping Station." 150 metres over-right (south) are the buildings of Staunch Farm.

Skirt this impenetrable fortress on your left, then find a path which threads between the trees south-eastwards for 250 metres.

Once cover is broken, you will note a thick copse ahead. Walk towards this 400 metres south-eastwards across an open field and one kilometre on from the plank and handrail you will arrive at a place they call Wormingford Mere (#27).

Two things are of note here. The first is that about 50 metres west of the mere you have entered in to the Dedham Vale Area of Outstanding Natural Beauty (AONB), the second is that they really don't want you to be here! Signage informs you quite clearly that you are not welcome and, "if you are reading this sign then you are trespassing" well ok.

To the right is Wormingford Mere - Keep out!

Skirting around the west and north of the mere, by the way, whilst slightly "off-pathing" gives more lovely Stour views, but if you've seen enough of those already, no worries.

With the mere to the left, the path carries on down an open field for 200 metres, dropping slightly then climbing. There is a lone broad-leafed tree to rest beneath and slake one's thirst, then another kissing-gate (metal this time) and in to the next field. Here things climb further still which means views open out as much as they ever can do in Essex, or indeed any of the eastern counties.

The Slaken-thirst Oak!

The Essex Alps!

We are aiming for Church Road, Wormingford 600 metres to the east. Continuing with the SVP, it heads right before offering a number of choices including jutting back leftwards. Whilst that goes nearer to the river, you will not see said river. It goes near, but not to Wormingford Mill. There is little to be gained, other than being closer to the river, so having turned right to begin with turn left (but not hard left) walk east across Lodge Hills and keep on that path, eschewing a right-hand turn and head towards the woodland in front.

Head for the wooded slopes

The path disappears in to the wood and then emerges rather wonderfully into a churchyard. This is St. Andrews of Wormingford (#28). A step offers you exit from said churchyard when it is locked up and you should now turn left, admiring the quaint old houses and the most steep-pitched mansard roof you are ever likely to see, on the left about 100 metres on, before turning right, between the pillars.

This path leads you for just shy of 100 metres to the old school. This quaint little cob-walled building has been somewhat blemished by its various accretions, but in this setting amongst the trees and fields, with a quaint (also cob) wall running along its side, it is a place of sweet memories.

The building has no lost its educational use and is now the "Wormingford Community Education Centre."

To its right, a path leads up to a field and kissing gate and beyond this the path charges east for 100 metres.

This then curls around north (left) and right (east) just south of woodland. 200 metres on it arrives at The Grange on Colletts Chase. Just south of a pond called "Pond Bay" The path dips south-east (right-ish), then east (left) and is called Garnon's Chase.

Garnon's Chase

As it strikes north (left) it is next to one of two reservoirs. A long, straight, tree-lined path north (600 metres) leads to Garnon's itself, now right down School Lane for another 600-odd metres, first east then south-east. Then, just as it turns hard right (south) a pair of footpath signs present themselves, choose the left one.

This goes north-east, then turning left and re-joining the SVP in woodland.

School Lane

A small wooden bridge crosses a stream, then a larger, metal sided structure the Stour itself. We need to linger in Suffolk a little while.

The little bridge   The big one (into Suffolk)

Turning right straight away, and with the river unusually on the right (for we have crossed the border) moving from one field to the next and 400 metres along is Wiston or Wissington Mill (#29). This is a Grade II* listed building and I leave its credentials to Historic England's disposal: "A fine C18-C19 timber-framed and weatherboarded watermill no longer in use." This building is the "latest" iteration, with records of a mill on this site going back to the 1600s. Indeed, the mill-race contains Tudor brickwork. You won't be able to see this of course, and in fact the closest you will get is the view of the house rather than the mill itself 100 metres down the driveway. At least the aspect is open, so you may stare straight in and admire, to an extent.

Soon after, turn right as footpath signs squeeze you between two lines of field fences ("squeeze" is an exaggeration, the gap is about three metres – "corral" then) past some of the mill's lesser if still pleasant buildings.

This takes you 100 metres, before you cross over the mill stream (confusingly labelled "the Stour" on some maps), then left in a similar corral for about another 100 metres.

And finally, after literally minutes away, an impossibly narrow but high-sided single span wooden bridge takes you back over the Stour proper and once more in to Essex.

Turn left after the crossing (the signposts are clear) over a flat wooden ditch bridge and through woodland in a north-easterly direction for about 200 metres as it circumnavigates a pond

Finally a grassy path takes you out, through a field gate, on to the very narrow Water Lane and left. for 800 metres.

Past Brook House, The Nurseries on the right. At some points there is a bit of verge, but for the last couple of hundred metres the considerate landowner has shaved a friendly swathe behind the tussock and this takes us past – of all things reindeer!

Over a little wooden ditch-bridge and on to the A134 and a careful crossing is required. As can be seen from the photograph, the footpath sign clearly indicates that the path carries on.

Just out of view is a metal gate, through which a field edge walk of 350 metres takes us all the way to the "Stour". Here, it seems to have split in to two channels, but the "southern "river" is in fact a flood relief channel. This was part of the major works when the bypass and the new bridge on the A134 was built in 1969. It forms the current county boundary – but this wasn't always so.

The Bridge in to "Suffolk"

Life-long Naylander Chris Hunt tells the tale of the three houses (Bridge House on the left, Riverside on the right) on Horkesley Road (plus Lock Cottage), where the children, whilst they had gone to Nayland Primary School with the rest of the villagers, were then sent off six miles south to Colchester for secondary school whilst their friends were sent nine miles in the opposite direction to Sudbury. All this because they were in a different county. The Essex and Suffolk (County Boundaries) Order 1989 came in to force on 1st April 1990 and changed all that.

Two "Suffolk" houses that used to be in Essex!

What had been done to Ballingdon was now done to these houses and (less explicably) the field north of Horkesley Road which runs all the way to the northern branch of the river.

Until 1990, therefore, the backs of Bear Street, with their lovely riverside gardens, were literally feet away from the neighbouring county. Was that more the reason for the change?

Nayland local Chris Hunt points to the field of contention

No matter, the bridge crossed, turn right here on the Horkesley Road, past the turncoat houses and we're done. Now for a drink and snack at the Anchor Inn, Nayland (#30).

This is the only one of the nights where there is no easy place to stop. Walking on to Dedham (where the nearest on-route B&B appears to be) would be punishing. So, a taxi it is to…somewhere for bed for the night!

Why not try Colchester, just six miles down the road where there is a Premier Inn hotel by a river next to an historic park, miles of Roman wall, a gurgling river and Europe's largest Norman keep? Tomorrow we go in to the heart of Constable Country.

Day Three – From Nayland to Dedham (7 miles)

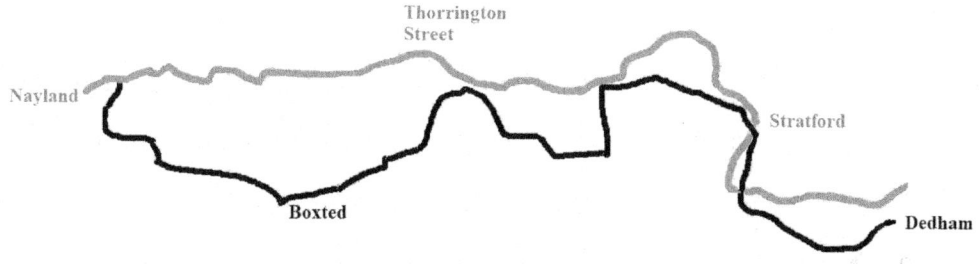

The shorter day of the four, with a slow start and later walk given the logistics of getting back to Nayland (which will probably mean a taxi, although there is a bus service).

Once leaving Nayland, most of the walk is on country lanes, with some footpaths. Picturesque Boxted is the only built-up part of the journey until Stratford, just a mile and a half from the end. And then is lovely Dedham, the jewel of the Stour.

Day Three Part One

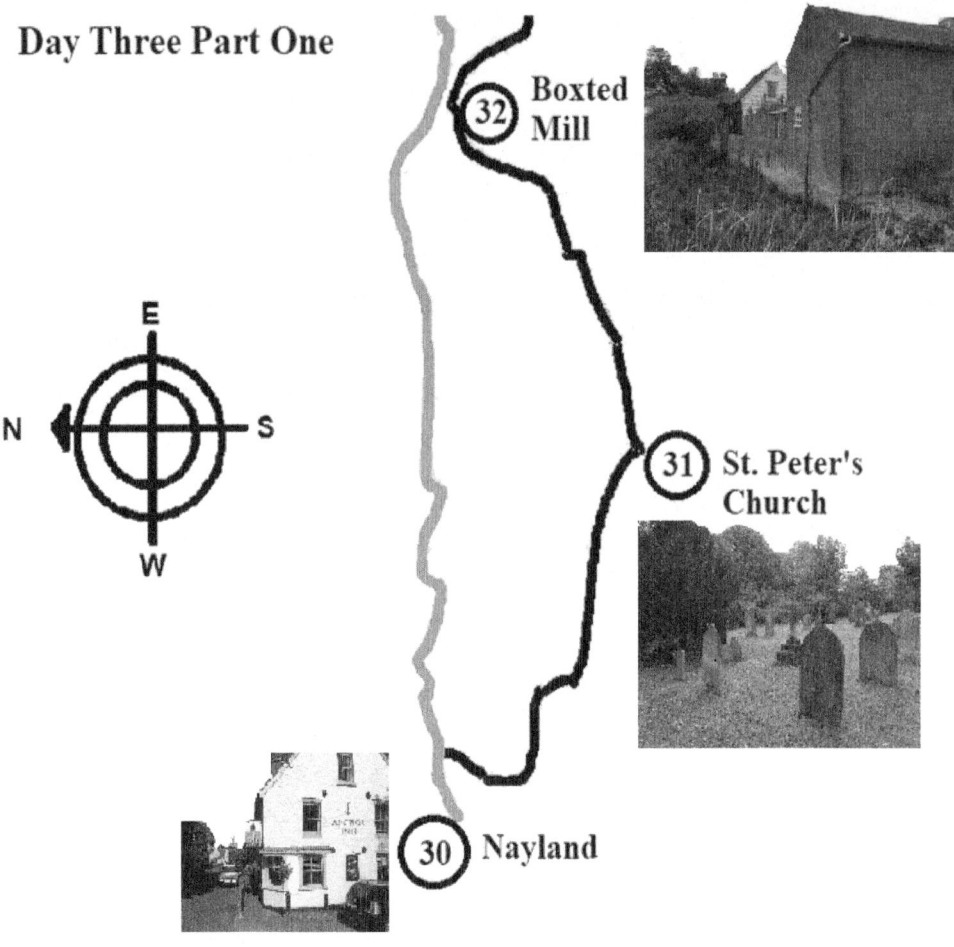

- 32 Boxted Mill
- 31 St. Peter's Church
- 30 Nayland

From the hotel (if you did opt to stay at the Premier) take a stroll through the adjacent historic Norman Castle and its award-winning park which is bi-sected by the longest stretch of Roman Wall (bar Hadrian's) in Britain. After the Castle Park and its ornamental gates is the beautiful war memorial Just beyond this is town, the High Street and there are other things to delay you, however this is straying too far from the original mission.   100 yards to the right is a taxi rank.

From here take a cab back to Nayland. If the timing is right after a slow morning, why not have a drink?

Taking The Anchor as your starting point, turn left out of it then left again over that arched bridge and back in to Essex.

Hang a left and the path curls nicely around with the river for 500 metres or so. It appears that some of this is a permissive as opposed to Public Right of Way, meaning the owner gives access but may, at any given time, withdraw access (often for one day a year) in order to ensure rights of way do not accrue! Here the river is clearly visible at times and, at the time of writing, was virtually dry.

Just by Horkesley Lock Bridge (another arched thing – closed at the time of writing for repairs - which leads north to Suffolk and the ancient monument Court Knoll) a gate and footpath sign invite us to jut off over to the right for about 150 metres.

This disappears in to a thin band of trees, through a metal gate and over a narrow wooden footbridge with handrails both sides. Now emerging on to a road, Park Road. Nearby a sign alerts us to the Pops Bridge Borehole Source.

Turn left, the next kilometre and a bit is road and verge walking, generally hedged on the left and a little more open on the right.

400 metres along a footpath pulls off to the right (ignore it!) 200 metres more, the road drops a little and, having bent around to the left, just past a field gate, Park Road becomes Burnt Dick Hill (stoppit!). All is placid, all is bucolic, all is still, all is a bit uneventful.

A field gate to the left, a pole barn to the right, various other bits and pieces.

The path bends around right and climbs slightly, shortly after a white field gate a generous green swathe opens out on the left and there is the most pleasant mansarded Bundooks Hill House.

Just a little way along, two pairs of more prosaic cottages, a turn right and just 100 metres later is a footpath on the left, by Boxted Hall Farm (the impressive Boxted Hall is hidden behind topiary just next door, you might be able to just sneak a peek).

Take the footpath, this is the Essex Way. Pass the black barns and other buildings, arching around to the right between the buildings and across the gravel and the path breaks out into the open. A hedge on the left almost hides the finger post, but turn left just after the hedge.

Closer up, we see this is the Essex Way. We follow the field edge path for 200 metres. We turn left and pick a path between the churchyard of St. Peter's Church (#31) and its separate Commonwealth War Graveyard.

The path emerges on to Church Street. Turn left. This part of Boxted is a delightful little hamlet, with something of the chocolate box about it. After a group of four pebble-dashed terraced houses, carry on right, do not be tempted into turning left. The delights continue.

About 500 metres from the church, the road hitches left (north) at Lower Farm. This is Lower Farm Road. A footpath right would be a shorter route, but is further from the river and would deny you a lovely water mill.

Lower Farm Road, first north then east, then north then east, is a 1km walk, no longer an official footpath, at times is narrow, the odd country house popping up, open fields over the Stour valley to the left, then finally Boxted Mill (#32).

What a quintessentially Constablesque visual offering. Not quite Flatford, but perhaps not so terribly far off (although it is private and views of it are not so up close and personal). The best views are across from the bridge over the Stour itself, this is a metal and not so pretty thing, but past it are things of beauty.

Day Three Part Two

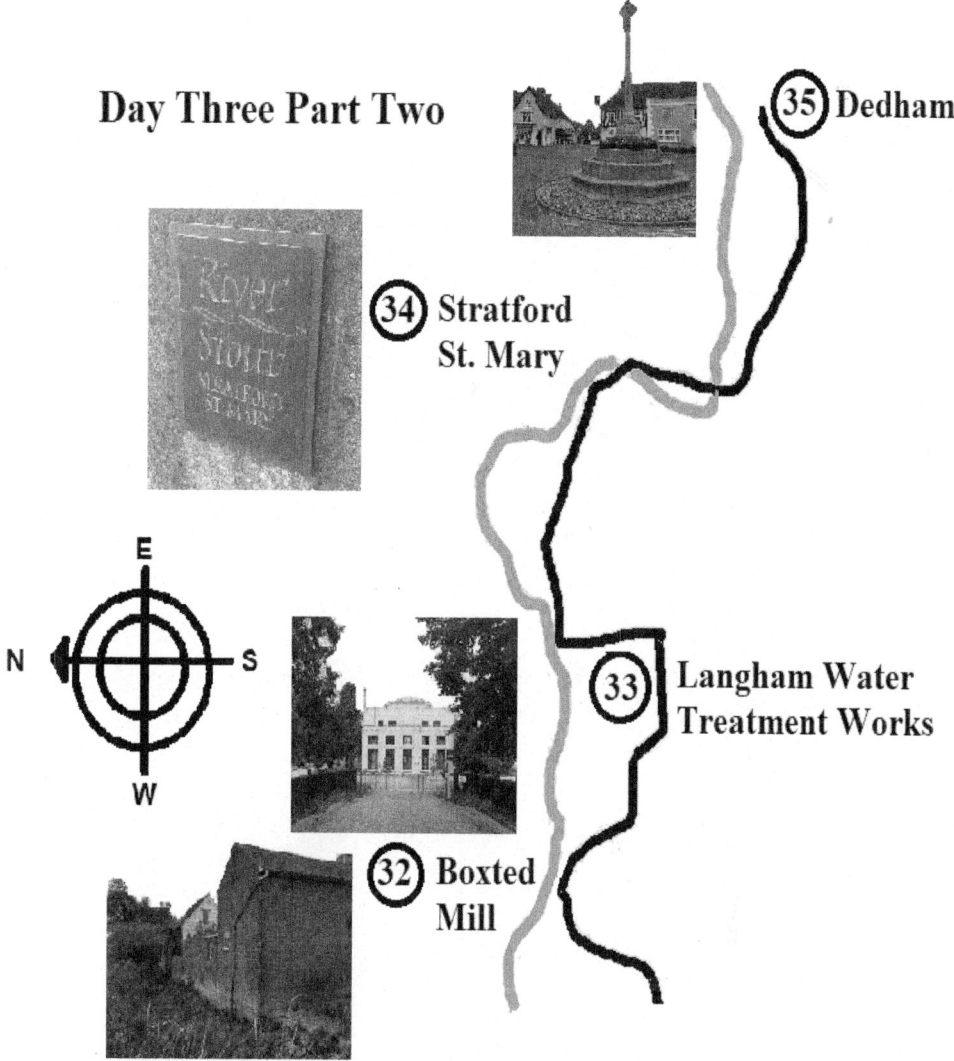

35 Dedham

34 Stratford
St. Mary

33 Langham Water
Treatment Works

32 Boxted
Mill

A fine brick wall curls off of Lower Farm Road, on to the poetically monikered Sky Hall Hill. An old signpost offers us a choice of destinations, ignoring Boxted Church, Colchester, Stoke and Higham, we make for Boxted Cross.

A pink house on our right looks across Sky Hall Hill and a tended lawn and has enviable views of the slow-moving Stour. The road passes twice over a thin band of water which runs parallel with and away from, then back to the main Stour, creating an island split in to two chunks of 700 metres long, but never more than 100 metres wide.

As usual, a verge of varying (sometimes to very little) width is our companion as Sky Hall Lane bends left and that little strand follows along on our left. 300 metres from the mill, the road bends right (due south) and soon enough a metal pailing fence is on our left, and stays with us for 150 metres. What is it protecting?

Large buildings heave in to view and the pailings are, disappointingly, replaced by close-board. Red brick wall and cottage over right as views open up over left, it almost looks industrial.

150 metres since the close-board and a turn to the left brings us on to High Lift Villas Road, what a name! The road is indeed filled with villas on its right-hand side, but on the left it is soon clear that we are at a waterworks, the Langham Water Treatment Works (#33) no less.

This is a politely composed commercial industrial building, probably from the 1920s. Moving along, on the right is the modest brick building hosting Quinta Raddison Limited, apparently "Procurement Specialists for Heavy Industry Worldwide", well.

Beyond that is the car park of the same and as the waterworks fizzle out on the left, that is the end of any meaningful action on High Lift Villas Road. Open country on both sides for the next 100 metres or so until, with a water tower in view, and a quaint wooden sign to the left showing Water Lane, the road sweeps around to the right, as do we.

This hems the (infiltration plant??) for 250 metres due south (offering glimpses of the tower, through railings and a "Keep Out!" sign). This body of water covers 3 hectares, but cannot be seen. This is a very narrow bit of road and you may think to actually walk the right-hand field just inside the hedge. At the end of this, a T-junction offers (as e'er it did) a left and right and it is left we go. Again a friendly field edge may offer itself for the next 500 metres as we eventually pass Docuras farm and farmhouse.

About 150 metres on from this is another T-junction and again we take a left. Marked as a footpath, this is in fact a tight single-track roads which leads 600 metres north to Low Lift Cottages. It will have become apparent that for the last half hour we have gone three sides of a square and travelled 1.3 miles to move just 0.6 miles! It is not unusual to have to circumnavigate immovable objects on country walks. Usually this might be a mountain or even a stubborn hill. Not so here, this is Essex, East Anglia. No, the immovable object is the water treatment works and reservoir which, for very good reason, one cannot simply cut across.

DOCURAS FARM ROAD

Low Lift Cottages are a small group of dwellings, presumably connected with workers at the neighbouring waterworks. Just past these houses are green equipment cabinets and the road goes rightwards, past another of those austere looking waterworks buildings.

We are near to the Stour now, and by turning off-piste left one can peek at a pretty little bridge and the river itself (along with various signs on the left, advising us how deep the hidden water is at the waterworks).

Turning back on to the road we were on, this shows an opening ahead which takes us across fields. A signpost informs us that we have rediscovered the St. Edmunds Way.

This path is as straight as a die for almost 700 metres, crossing two fields. As the river disappears from 150 to 250 metres over-left, the land is more elevated on the right and our path heads closer to the river.

And at this point we turn right and re-join the Stour Valley Path/St. Edmund Way/Stour Valley Path. We are heading towards a lone, yellow rendered farm (Broomhouse). Near to Broomhouse, a small patch of trees emerges to the left, and towards the end of these, the path turns left on to another field, then right. This goes on for about 600 metres, generally easterly (isn't everything on this jaunt?) much of which is alongside (though often blocked from view) a small lake which seems to take water from the Stour? Manmade?

After this, the next 300 metres give largely riverside walking, which is the most we have seen for a long time. Some of this is quite breath-taking in a Constablesque way – rolling pasture, grazing cattle, drooping trees reflected in glassy water. Maybe not outstanding, nor even natural (for in such a state, woodland would prevail) but certainly an Area qualifying for one of the last three letters of AONB.

Emerging from the wooded area, and through a kissing gate, the path arches away right-ish and leaves the river behind.

A diagonal field walk south-easterly for about 300 metres leads to another small wood, where a small metal gate leads to a little wooden bridge which will take us in to Suffolk for a while.

This is followed by another near a millpond area of water and we are in Stratford St. Mary (#34), turn right here and enjoy 200 metres of an attractive Suffolk village.

Near the end, on the right, is a pub, the Black Horse Inn. If you're thirsty, you know what to do.

Now the village runs out and there are 300 metres more of Suffolk, with the path on the right. This stretch is treed over, straight and largely featureless, save for a ponded area to the left half way along, which separates us from the hiss of the A12 just 50 metres away.

100 metres after this is the bridge which leads back in to Essex. And my what a scene from the bridge over to the right! The river is a placid glass and next to it an exquisite Tudor building with several ranges of clay-tiled roofs. This is Le Talbooth (it's got a French name, so it must be good) riverside restaurant.

This is not cheap, but the setting is simply breath-taking, manicured lawns swirl around it, the land banks up and the gentle hill are wooded. A range of outbuildings surround it of equal worth, a truly splendid re-entry back into the county of three swords.

Misleadingly just afterwards is the county sign for Essex and at this point it is advised to cross to the left, just in time for the path and road to swing around that way off of The Street and down on to the Stratford Road.

Soon enough the London – Great Yarmouth road – better known as the A12, is beneath our feet and the path goes on for 150 metres more, trees on all sides. Ahead is Dalethorpe House and across from this the land banks up sweetly with a tempting footpath sign to the right. However, what needs doing here is almost a doubling back.

At the Milsoms sign turn left and follow the road until you arrive at Milsoms itself. This is an expensive overnight option. Just opposite the entrance, where the hedgerow ends next to a lighting bollard, is our footpath, almost ashamedly hiding its face.

Spot the sign!

Through woodland for 100 metres, with a brief gap and the gardens of Dalethorpe open to view and, better than that, are glimpses of the river.

Then another clump of trees, at the end of which is a kissing gate, next to a wooden fence. Beyond this a once-proud National Trust sign for Bridge Farm, lying on its side.

Across 200 metres of an, at times, muddy field. Cows are in attendance, but far enough away so as not to cause too much disquiet. Just at the end of this though, a surprise as a mound of beef waddles just in front of me from my left, having joined the throng from a diagonally-adjoining field. Escape is quick, though, through a kissing gate which urges one to a field on the left and to safety.

This hems a field of crop for 500 metres, mostly due east-south-east and slipping away from our river (**confession – if, just before the border crossing one had taken a footpath to the left, it would have been possible to follow a river path for a mile.

This would have had the obvious advantage of being just that, a river walk, and also of emerging near The Boathouse – teas, coffees, snacks and...well....boats, as well as the lovely Dedham Mill. However, we are unashamedly looking at the south side of the river, there will be plenty more river walking tomorrow and walking the Essex side allows you to see all of lovely Dedham. So there **).

Anyway.

The field walking comes to an end at a red-roofed black barn and a narrow lane winds past Dedham's allotments and out on to B1029 (High Street). Every building is to speak of.

Across the road are the Assembly Rooms, a wooden structured building dating in part from the mid-18th century and largely restored in the early 20th century. Here the Dedham Village Players were rehearsing their production of "Pressure" by David Haig, the stage all set up like a war-room, huge weather charts filling out the wall.

Left from the footpath is all the glory of Dedham (#35). Clare is a lovely place, quite a bit bigger than Dedham but with some its loveliness diluted amongst the ordinary. Dedham doesn't have that. It is pretty much all lovely wherever you turn. Of all the places on the Stour, Dedham bears the crown.

There are many Georgian properties, some older mansarded houses, others warped and older still, little lanes with yet more of the quaint, traditional shopfronts, pleasing and surprising patches of green, the lovely tower of Dedham Parish church, the War Memorial in Royal Square.

There are some whimsical touches. The Co-op is rebranded here as "HIGH CLASS GROCERS" with the "Cop-operative" part of the name hidden in smaller font in the middle. *Closer inspection revealed that this Co-op sells exactly the same as any other – right down to the crisps and fizzy drinks!*

For a detour, turning left here would take you to Dedham Mill which is nice enough, but maybe in the context of all else, not to be bothered with.

Where the day ends depends where you are staying, of course. The afore-mentioned Co-op is a few doors past the Sun Inn, which has rooms. The photographs here show its sumptuous features, roaring fire and quirky fittings, including a table shaped like a book and buckets for urinals. The Sun Inn recently featured in the "i" newspaper as one of Britain's best pubs "The Sun Inn, Dedham, Suffolk" needless to say a letter was sent in asking for a correction – which was not published. Next to the Co-op is the Essex Rose Tea Room, run by Wilkin & Sons (you know the nice jam, it's from Tiptree, just down the road) Just opposite the Co-op is the Marlborough Head public house and three-star hotel. Behind this is the Tallow Factory and further back in the village (not far from the Assembly Rooms) is One Threadneedle Street.

An alternative could be to push on past the war memorial as the thoroughfare changes its name to Brook Street, past yet more Georgian loveliness and Dedham Art & Craft Centre (worth a visit and a cuppa if you get there before 5) and down the path to the left and 150 metres up to Dedham Hall. This B&B also offers a series of art courses.

Day Four – From Dedham to Harwich (14 miles)

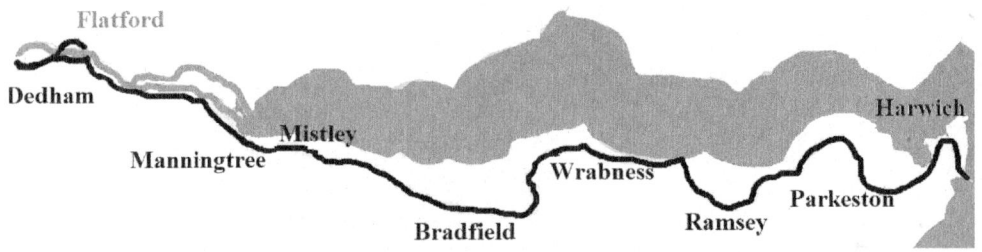

The final day. The river is with us for most of it, we say goodbye to one Area of Outstanding Natural Beauty and another which should be. Today is long and full of wonders, a cheeky nip across the border to Flatford, the first smell of the briny, the tide, the fine Stourside town of Manningtree, beach huts and a windmill and finally old Harwich as we reach the sea.

Day Four Part One

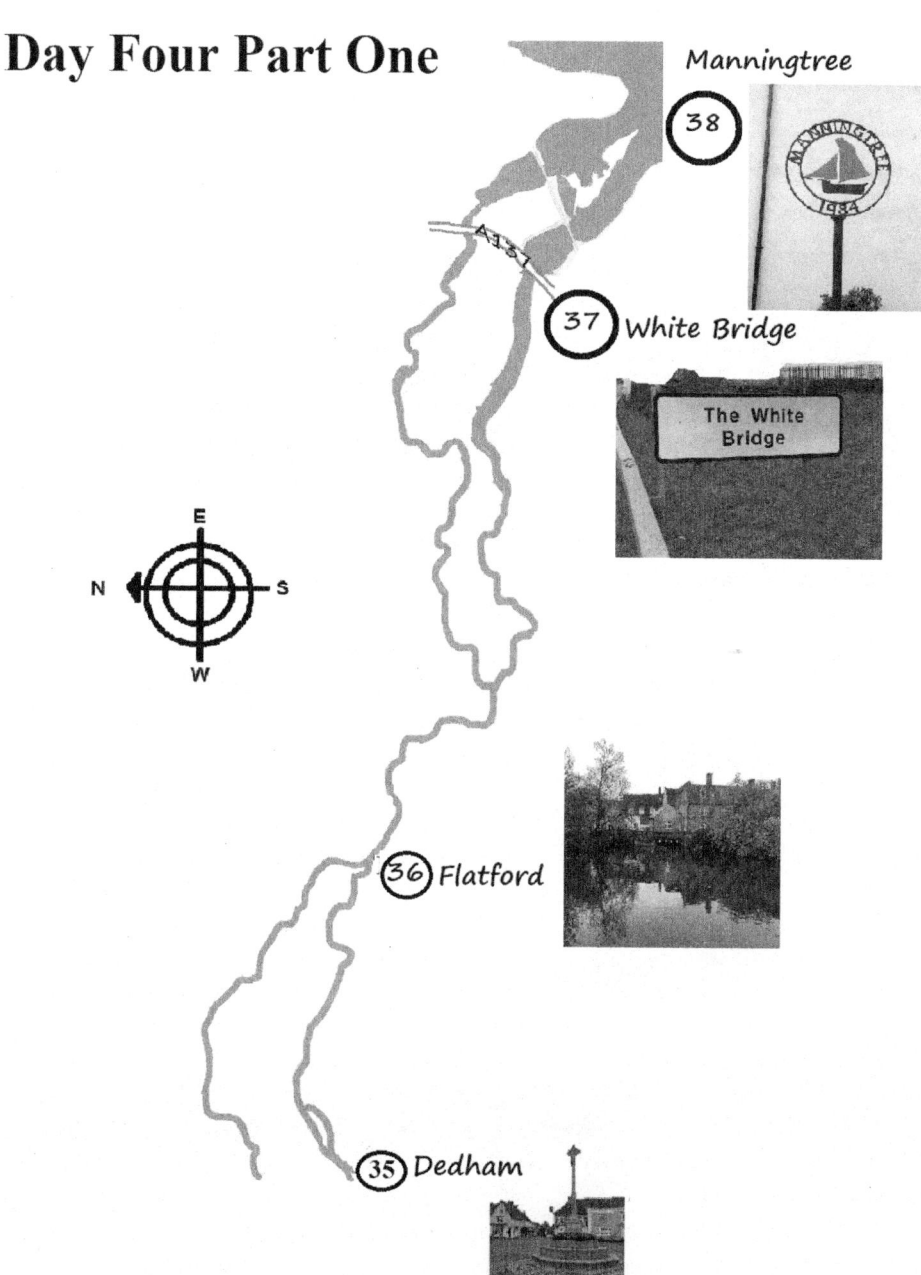

Manningtree

38

37 White Bridge

The White Bridge

36 Flatford

35 Dedham

Wherever you slept, by way of reference have that turning to Dedham Hall in mind.

Where the path goes off of Brook Street, another forks off right from it, directed towards Dedham Hall *Business Park*. In 600 metres this will have us at the Stour, and there we will stay for several miles.

A word of warning – 150 metres in there is a multi-fingered post which shows "Flatford 1.7 miles" and is pointing in the general, easterly, direction of said landmark. However, that route (apart from being longer) would actually take you across the fields and nowhere near the river. Having made that mistake and doubled back, the same post has a finger pointing in the general direction we had already been going – north-east, so regroup and go forth.

Shortly after said wooden wayfinder, the path disappears rather splendidly into a sylvan tunnel, where each specimen curls over to form a green roof.

This continues for almost 200 metres in a die-straight line until things open up at an un-gated field entrance next to a pointless kissing gate, emblazoned with that Stour Valley Path sign.

200 metres more, a sign for Dedham Hall tells us we are in National Trust territory and there is a set of wooden gates and fences on a concrete pad which crosses a tiny outpouring tributary.

This is Dedham Old River and its eponymous weir.

Dedham Old River is an important marker in terms of where Essex ends and Suffolk begins and a clue is in its name. This dried up old watercourse is the boundary between the two counties which suggests it may have been the original course of the Stour, or one of two strands which has since diminished? Pass! Either way, it means that the next three-quarters of a mile, whilst still on the Essex *side* of the Stour, will actually be in the other county.

Hereabouts, and in particular at the next gate along, the going can be treacherously muddy and, on our visit, was only passable by clever use of the gate itself as an impromptu swing.

This part of the walk, though, is pure and Constablesque, in fact we've used that adjective before, It is Constabelian, these are the very fields JC trod and set down his easel (or at least his sketch book, for later painting in his London studio) with flat pastureland on left and right, banking up slightly about a mile from the river on both sides, cows grazing and a perfect peace pervading. Trees have been pollarded with the result of spiny multi-stemmed creatures leaning sleepily on the lush grass.

This area is popular for kayakers too. Chris Jones from Felixstowe has been paddling the Stour for years. For him, this stretch of the river is the very quintessence of all that England's lowland countryside has to offer.

For those of us on dry land, the Stour views open up and do not close, but new and gentle bends in the river give surprising new aspects. The stillness of the river and the way in which it broadens here and there make it feel like a lake. Stands of trees are seen twice thanks to nature's mirror and you can implicitly understand why Constable chose to do what he did and share all of this with the world. Thank God he did, it gave the land a status which led it to receive a high level of protection as an Area of Outstanding Natural Beauty.

This has helped to stem the tide of what has been dumped on so much of the rest of Essex. Constable understood that times were changing, with the belching chimneys and satanic mills scarring England forever, and his celebration of his little corner of England helped to preserve it for the ages. Thank you, John Constable R.A.,

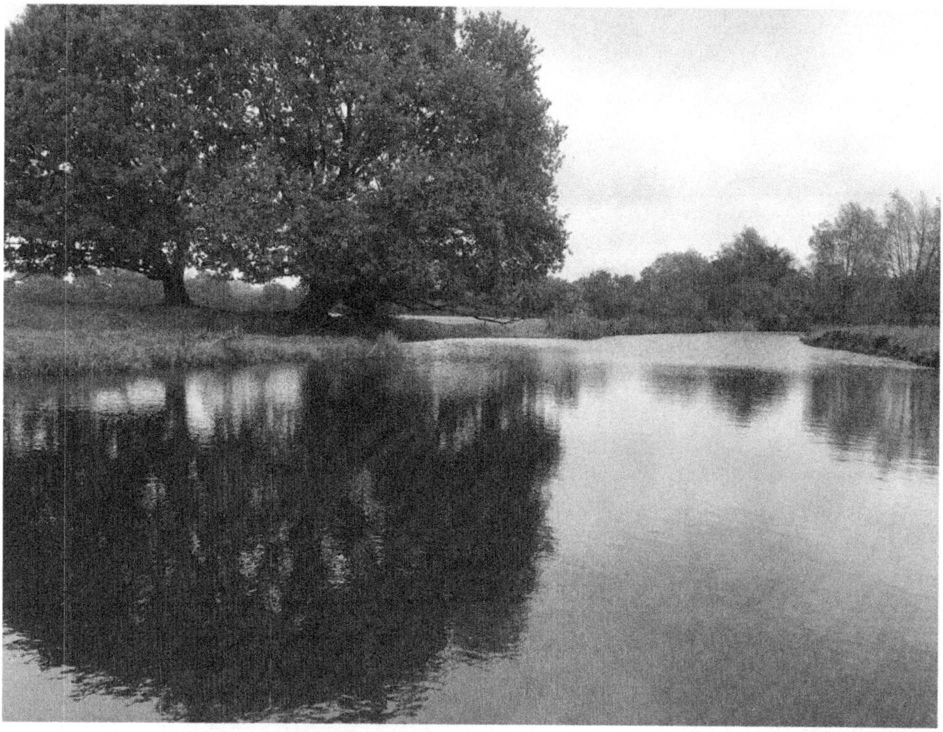

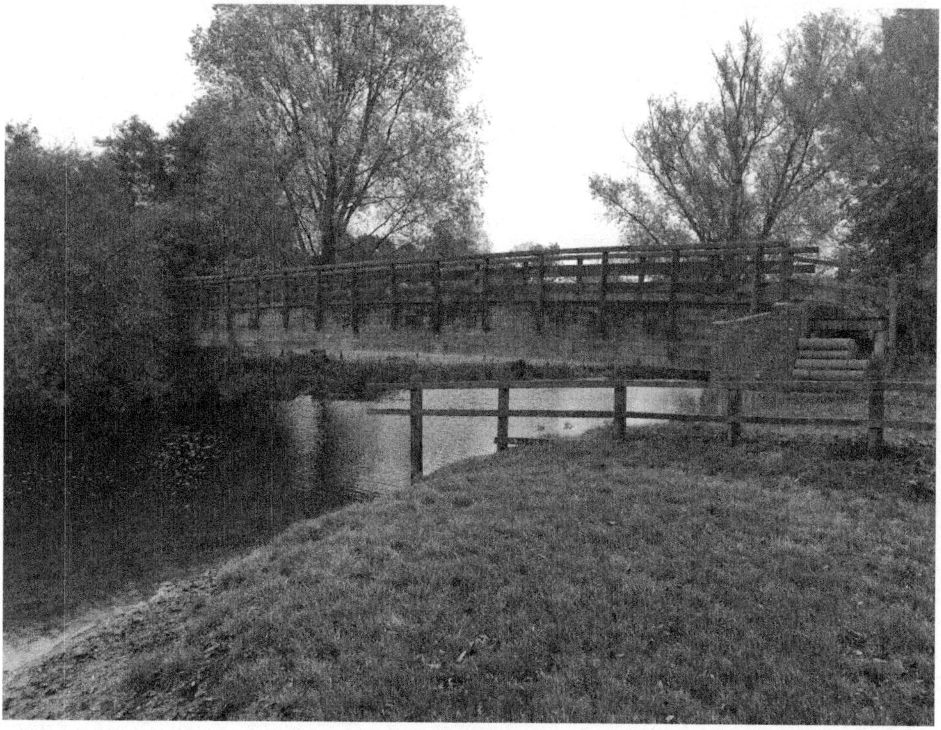

300 metres or so from our joining of the river path is Fen Bridge, a wooden structure rebuilt in 1983 and carrying a plaque in a place you can barely read in memoriam to Keith Turner.

150 metres on from this, it is important to stay close to the bank as a narrow channel/tributary threads its way north from the Dedham Old River and re-joins the mother Stour through a small concreted culvert.

If you're caught in the middle of the field, this channel is too wide to leap and you will have to walk 100 metres to the next crossing point. So just stick to the waterside, which is what this is all about in any event.

250 metres on, the river widens as a tributary comes in from the left. The maps show this as nothing more or less than a stream which links the Stour to another river just 200 metres north – also called the Stour.

The river is complex and braided at this point, these two arms of the same watercourse having parted company near the A12 two miles west, before coming together again shortly.

Along the banks are the odd tree, and some are indeed very odd indeed. Apart from the earlier-mentioned spiky pollards are some whose crooks have been exposed to soil erosion by wind and water, leaving enchanted arborial arches, just tall enough for pixies to stand beneath.

A few hundred metres and a few river bends later and the buildings of Flatford appear on our left (#36).

It would be utterly churlish, not to say silly, not to take advantage of the facilities (remember, Dedham and breakfast was a while ago) – coffee, cake, a wee. It's all here.

As for the history of the place, this is Constable HQ. There is the wooden bridge across to the East Bergholt side, there is Bridge Cottage. Next to this is the café, and just beyond is lovely Flatford Mill and Willy Lott's Cottage. To the left of said cottage is the National Trust building. This spot is worth a couple of hours, an hour or just half – depending on your time constraints. If the target is Harwich, then sustenance and, erm, convenience, may have to do.

Crossing back over the bridge, the next point of interest is Flatford Lock. New gates were installed in 2014.

Beyond this is a bench remembering "Frank and Mae". And what a lovely view they have as we take one last look across the river to Flatford Mill.

Pressing on and 400 metres later, Essex is regained after three-quarters of a mile in alien territory. We cross another strand of water called the "River Stour", this is an extension of "Dedham Old River". A narrow concrete bridge, with warning signs that the bridge is unsound! (for vehicles).

Just after this is a kissing gate and a National Trust sign and a multi-finger post. We take the middle finger (!) i.e. that pointing left, the Permissive Footpath to Manningtree, which is just 1.4 miles away.

This edges back towards the Stour for 300 metres until we almost re-join it, passing through a kissing gate. 100 metres to our left is the hauntingly-named Judas Gap Weir. Just along from this, the pylons appear and crackling can be heard overhead.

Judas Gap Wier

One meander later, the path begins to hug the river and this is the case for another mile. The river valley is flat and our Stour is now clearly tidal, large expanses of mud appearing as the river widens.

The river in this location, although this cannot be told from our vantage point, is still two channels – the lesser one being 400 metres to the north. To the right, trains thunder along the London-Norwich line.

By the time the Cattawade Bridge Sluice is reached, with life-belts and warning signs not to climb the structure, the salt and mud of the sea can be smelt for the first time on the whole journey.

The last half mile passes without feature, except for a set of farm buildings on the Suffolk side, until the grassy path takes us to the pink Marsh Barn, a self-catering place given four stars by Enjoy England.com.

That is the last point of reference until the White Bridge (#37), a bridge which is – wait for it – white (well, the rails are anyway), the last crossing point of the Stour (apart from the rail bridge 200 metres to the south).

The footpath carries on over this and to the other side and by this point the AONB designation has given up. Now the river walking continues on a levee, with fields to the right and sizzling cables overhead.

Soon enough a brick tunnel gives access below the railway line and the last way of crossing from Essex to Suffolk other than by boat is gone.

The path is elevated now, and soon it is clear that a northern channel is merging with our one. Finally, amidst the gloop, the Stour is united.

What follows is hardly salubrious. Whilst maltings lie ahead, what lies on the right and close by is a set of industrial buildings, single-storey, red brick, modern. Places of employment, necessary employment, special for that but, on a walk where dreams are sought, unremarkable on the eye.

Shipping containers, piled one on to the other, also fill the right-hand vista, but teasels and single mast boats angled jauntily in the mud vie for our attention on the riverside.

The memories of David Townes and Henry William Hughes gaze out across the briny and these are the last voices of the wilderness as, finally, we reach a town, the first Essex town in forty miles of walking our river.

It is also England's smallest town, Manningtree (#38). With only 900 people according to the 2011 census, this claim is on shaky ground, with Fordwich in Kent weighing in with considerably fewer people.

Day Four Part Two

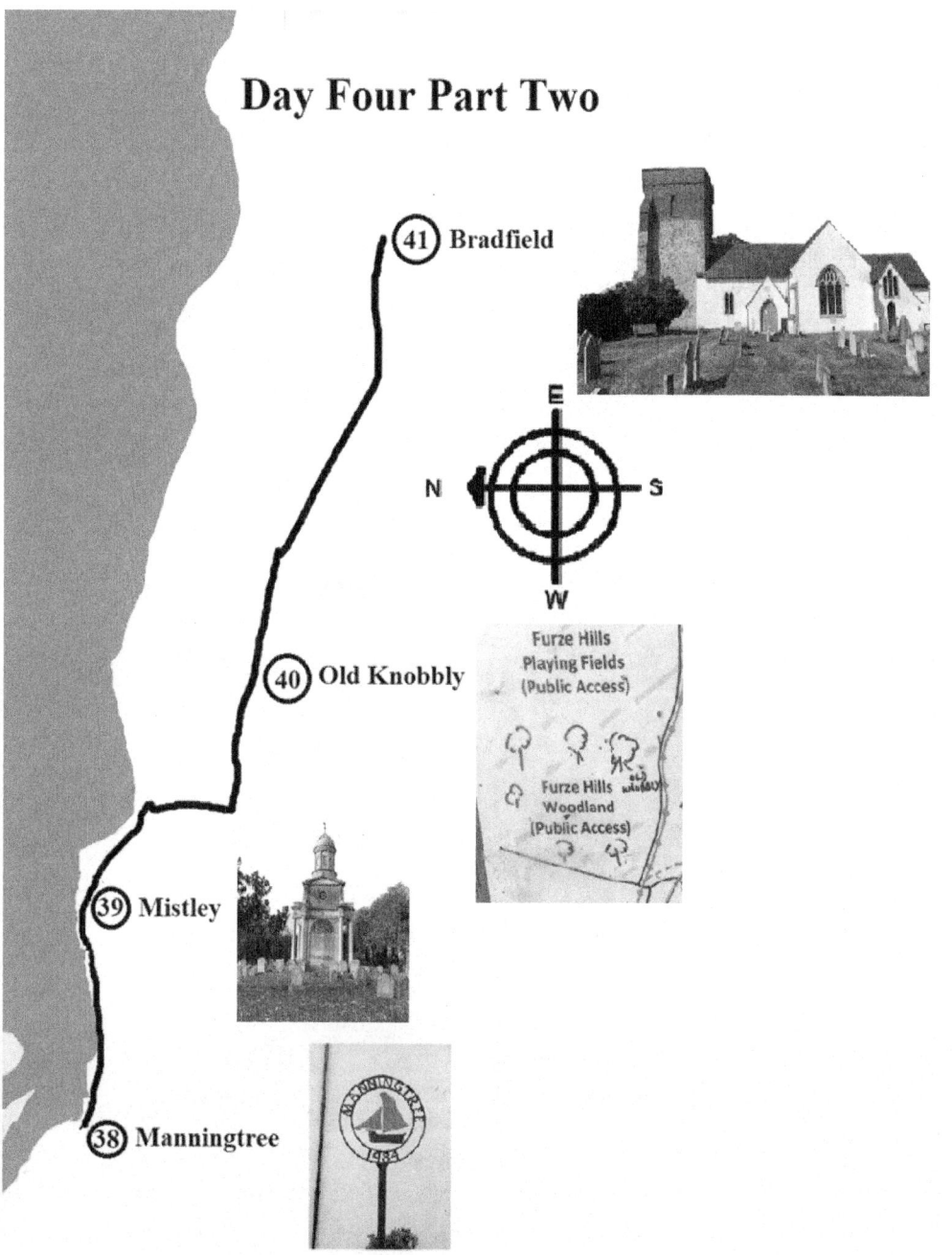

41 Bradfield

E
N   S
W

Furze Hills
Playing Fields
(Public Access)

40 Old Knobbly

Furze Hills
Woodland
(Public Access)

39 Mistley

38 Manningtree

With the co-operative store on your right, by a set of cream-coloured, riverside, residences of Maltings Wharf on the left, there is a set of steps with a metal handrail, which reach down in to the grass and a gravelly path heading left at the bottom. Soon can be seen a community noticeboard and, turning left at said board, the Riverside Health Centre.

Turning left just after this, we emerge on to Station Road and immediately stumble upon the Skinners Arms. Manningtree has a pleasing air, with mainly old buildings and bunting strung across the street.

About 150 metres from The Skinners is an oddity. Where High Street meets South Street, known locally as Market Cross, on the gable end of a red brick clothing shop "Togs" is the image of an ox strung up on high for all to see. This is in frame form, so you can see inside it and there within a round object lies inside the stomach. Bizarre out of context.

However, this is the Manningtree Ox. Yes, it is this small town's proud claim that it gets a mention in Henry IV Part I, where Prince Hal compares Falstaff with 'a roasted Manningtree ox with a pudding in his belly'. Legend is that the bard may have passed through this way as a young actor, but this is unproven.

Besides its smallest town and Shakespeare links, Manningtree's other claim to fame is its association with that most heinous of coves, the Witchfinder General one Matthew Hopkins. During the unrest of the Civil War, Hopkins and his associates saw to the deaths of 300 "witches" in just over one year between 1644 and 1646 – more than in the preceding 160 years combined.

Put another way, of all the "witches" executed between the late 15th and early 18th centuries, Hopkins and co accounted for 60 per cent. What a nice man. The only bright point of the tale was that he died from tuberculosis aged only 27, so ha-ha.

There is no shortage of places to eat in Manningtree, The Mogul (Bangladeshi) and the exquisite Lucca Enoteca both just on the left being the pick. However,

Flatford was only about an hour ago and a complete blow-out might not be the best idea with still ten miles to go.

Just after Lucca's is The Crown. This lovely old pub has a gated carriage-arch through to the river. It is an option to pass through this and eat, drink, or just carry on with the walk, turning right at the bottom. If not, the building soon curls around leftwards anyway and will take us there – tie-plates and cottages, masts and the Suffolk bank filling the view.

Quay Street becomes The Walls and benches provide a place for rest. Here, also, is what can be described as a beach. It is just about possible to walk in sand and even make a sandcastle. Moving on, the impressive and politely-composed Brooks Maltings development is on the right and the wall gives way on the left to a soft grass as the sign advises that we are leaving Manningtree.

An old red-brick garden wall extends in to the distance on the right, but on the left is the first sign of a battle that has endured down the ages: Man versus Swan, or rather how to deal with the fact that people like feeding swans.

The black litter bin on the greensward gives us the opening exchange, a sign is all over it, advising: "Cars Kill Swans" further instructing us to feed the long-necked lovelies only in the river and NOT from the grass, and certainly not from our cars.

This has been a gathering point for Mute Swans, and occasionally the odd Bewick, for time beyond memory. Common thought is that they have been here since the seventeenth century when they would feed off the barley which blew off barges which sailed the Stour Estuary. They now number 200 plus and can be quite a handful.

They are, however, part of the folklore of these parts and much-loved, appearing on the logo for the village primary school and the crest for the rugby club

It also houses a few black swans, but these are apparently an accidental import. Originally from Australia they were probably part of a private collection and either escaped or were dumped here.

They seem to get on alright with the natives, but so far no grey swans have been reported.

To the right is Mistley Place (remember that long wall) and the tired old sign of Mistley Place Park, tea room and restaurant. This houses a variety of animals which had fallen upon hard times before finding salvation here. For some years this was a petting zoo, but the animals are no longer open for public visits – the tearooms, however, are five days a week (at the time of writing that's Wednesday to Sunday).

Easier to access than that, though, is the Al Fresco burger van, also offering hot dogs, bacon, chips and other health foods (not swan though).

Swan burgers anyone?

Across Mistley Place Park, views open up of the 19th century St Mary & St Michael's Church (in the parish of Mistley *with* Manningtree), whilst on the left just after a green bench remembering the long-lived local Len Harris, beaches begin to briefly form again and Oyster Catchers flit across the shore. Further progress is blocked by a sea wall atopped with the wooden fence of a house with a most enviable aspect on the world.

Lucky beggars!

Keeping said house to the left and eschewing the chance to turn left as bidden by an "Essex Way"-toting finger post, carry on, arrive in Mistley (#39) and be rewarded by what would appear to be the loveliest of follies. The twin cupolas are a visual joy and appear to belong in Brideshead Revisited.

But Mistley Towers are not a folly, they are the remnants of the church of St. Mary The Virgin and speak of ambition to turn Mistley in to a spa town like Brighton (so, yes, a folly after all). A Georgian church was built here in the early 18th century following the death of one Richard Rigby. His rich, politician son of the same name had the cupolated towers built in the 1770s, but to no avail. Long story short, it didn't work and the church is gone. The towers, however, are Grade I listed.

To stay faithful to the river, a left after the towers takes us to the grim industrial reality and the tale of a modern-day battle royal (access to the walls)

In September 2008, at the bequest of the Health and Safety Executive, owners Trent Wharfage erected a safety fence along the quay. A protest group was formed to object to the fence, claiming that it ended 500 years of free access to the water. After locals raised £35,000 to pay for legal advice a public enquiry was held, and Essex County Council ruled that the quay constituted a "village green". Locals hope this paves the way to the removal of the fence, on the grounds that it interferes with the public's enjoyment of the public space.

The water's edge - the place they don't want you to go!

The old Maltings Rails

Taking a right up past the ILECS building, brings you back on to High Street, by a lovely swan in a pond get-up, and just past the Mistley Thorn (a splendid pub and hotel).

Then are the Maltings (a maltings, by the way, is a building where cereal grain is converted into malt by soaking it in water, allowing it to sprout and then drying it to stop further growth. The malt is used in brewing beer, whisky and in certain foods. The traditional malt house was largely phased out during the twentieth century in favour of more mechanised production. That is a point to be made about Mistley, it is beautiful, but the air is thick with malt. If you do not like malt – do not live in Mistley!

And at the maltings a fresh wooden finger sign with the Essex Way badge on it urges us to turn right. This path leads down an improbably industrial aspect between high buildings and malt-filled lorries. At the end of this is a clinically metal gate two metres high, through which to pass and hang left.

Soon 18 concrete steps take us up to a tunnel beneath the railway line (which leads from Manningtree to Harwich). Down again and to some friendlier small white gates and out in to the field.

The path goes south for 500 metres across open fields, with the barrel-like plant of the Crisp Maltings to the left (nothing to do with crisps, that's just their name), then School Wood.

About 250 of those 500 metres along, the path transects an east-west path which is tree-lined and crossed via two kissing gates.

About 200 metres further, at a divergence of paths, turn left (east) and into a thin band of trees – keeping these (and the wire fences) to your left. At the next kissing gate a board makes it quite clear what is publicly accessible and what is not. Furze Hills Playing Fields to the west falling into the first category, and to the east "private woodland", well, no explanation required. The Essex Way cuts between the two.

As we enter the thick of the wood, 50 metres or so to the south (unseen) is Gamekeeper's Pond. About 150 metres in we come to Old Knobbley (#40).

This is actually just off our beaten track, but signposted. About 450 metres of woodland walking later, with glimpses of sports pitches and the village hall over-left two-thirds of the way along, the walk breaks out into the open.

Housing can be seen about 150 metres over to the left (the semi-detached of Rigby Avenue). Until recently, that cluster of 200 metres length was just about the only thing south of the B1352. Not any more though, as new housing goes up at a lick.

Some place level with where the new housing sits next to the old are the remains of St. Mary's Church, so the maps tell us – supposedly Matthew Hopkins was buried here. It wasn't clear what remains they may be or where exactly they were supposed to be, but none were visible on our walk.

With a black barn on the right, the field walking now comes to an end. By a field gate we pass a single, stylish dwelling on the right, then the path breaks out past a ranch fence and out on to Heath Road.

Right along here, very briefly until a tiny half-timbered bungalow is seen at the end of a row. This is called Wymarks. Just to the left of this is the footpath. Through kissing gates and running parallel with the bungalow and its garden across a little paddock, into a copse and another kissing gate, emerging from the trees over a collapsed stile.

In terms of suddenly opening out into a broad vista, this one tops the lot. From the confines of hedgerows and tiny lanes, suddenly all of north Essex (well, not all obviously) opens up over-left. Shaven yellow fields and the land sloping down to the estuary, the Suffolk Coast and Heaths AONB in full view.

The path strikes eagerly south-east for half a kilometre, following a weakly-defined field boundary towards a distant wood. Where that field ends, a thin line of trees cross left to right and the smallest of wooden plank bridges offers a crossing of an often dry stream. Closer inspection shows it to be adorned with some much-scuffed wayfinding badges, including "The Essex Way."

The path carries on for another 150 metres in the same direction, before meeting the next batch of trees and striking off ever so slightly leftwards in an almost perfectly east direction and then dropping slightly. This meets a field gate and finger sign and arrives amongst trees at Mill Lane.

The maps show the footpath and road to be in a straight line, although on arrival it does feel a bit more like a left turn.

With trees bowing over on both sides, this feels like a walk in the woods, the road is narrow and at times when the trees are winning there is no option but to walk in the road – all the more so as the knee rail on the left prevents easy access to the woodland under-layer (in which, however, is hidden a drop to the little watercourse – so stay on the dry side of things!)

Soon a parallel path appears on the left, however this leads to a small sub-station and the way through to the other end does not seem certain, so stick to the road. Opposite this, a stable building and two houses sit high on the brow of the tiny hill, fenced off by wire and rustic screening.

Those hill-top "houses" which are now to the right show themselves to be just one house "Mill House", an attractive old weather-boarded affair, with the other "house" being a grossly over-scaled double garage building with a generous provision of rooms above.

Whilst this dwelling does seem to be all on its own, it is only another 100 metres before Bradfield is with us. The first sign of humanity is on the left and is given over to those who were here yesterday, a tiny parish graveyard.

Now for 150 metres are various dwellings from the 1960s and later, with allotments to the right until the junction with The Street and Station Road is met. The latter, to the left, is the next part of the journey.

Bradfield Begins

Day Four Part Three

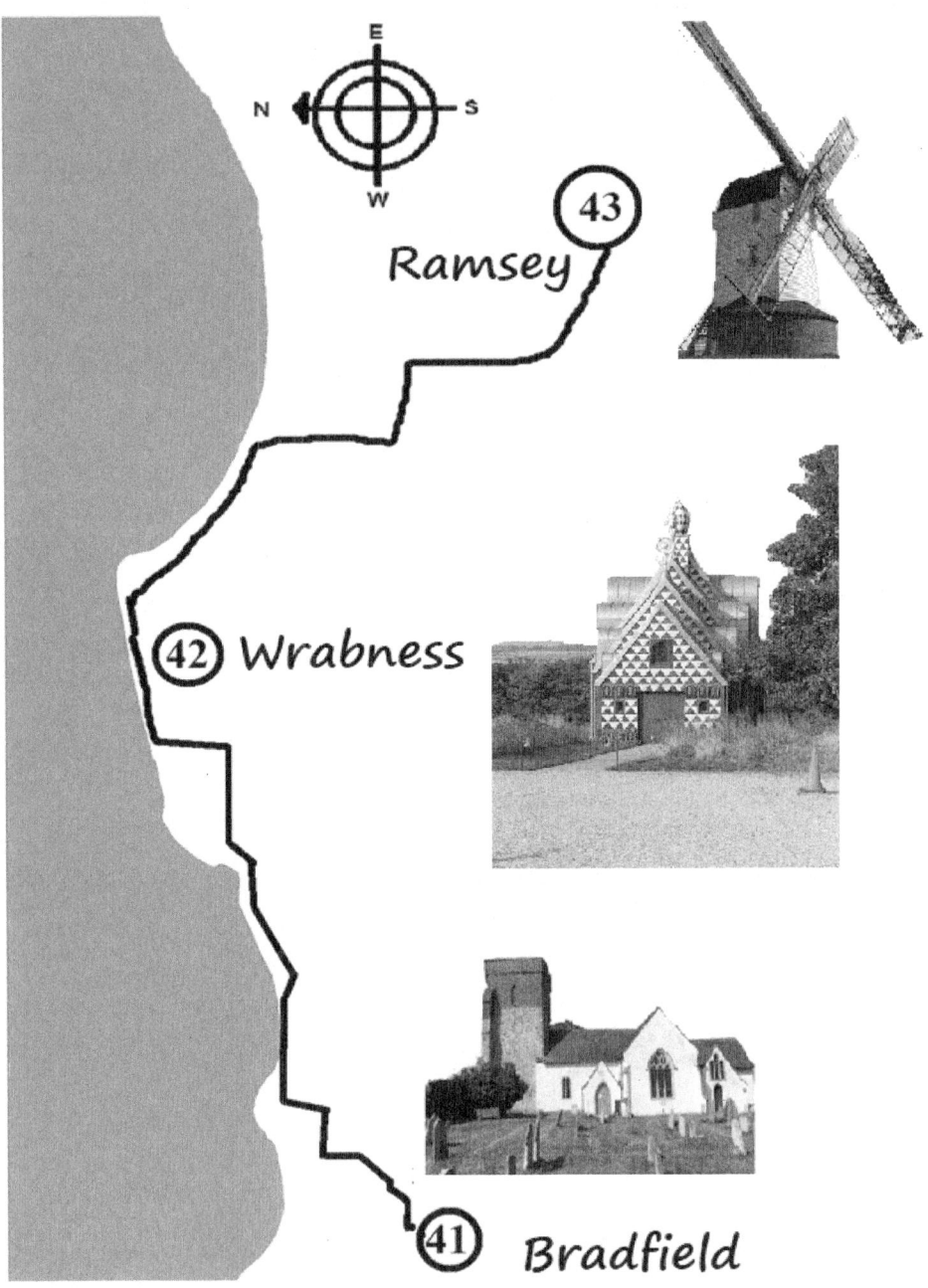

Ramsey 43

42 Wrabness

41 Bradfield

Mill Lane, whilst pleasant and quiet, is lined with ordinary housing stock and gives a fake first impression of what Bradfield (#41) has to offer. It is quite simply a charming little place. Eyes left and a range of quaint older buildings are on show (mixed in with some newer ones), many of them mansarded in the old Essex-Dutch way. The first are Lynden Cottage and Hallam Cottage on the left, and others such as Elderberry Cottage, right.

And then, through the most exquisite of lychgates, is the lovely church of St. Lawrence.

There are some 13th century remnants here and the place is the usual tale of building and re-building and re-use of materials. The cream-rendered nave and chancel are the oldest part, with the brick and rubble tower being 15th – 16th century.

Amongst the usual stain glass and memorial plaque offerings are two oddities which require comment. First is the "Grimston Helm" this is a funerary tribute to one Sir Edward Grimston, from a local family who died in 1580 and had been a diplomat in the service of Edward VI and Elizabeth I.

The second oddity is the grave of Squadron Commander Edwin Harris Dunning DSC RN of nearby Jaques Hall - the first man to land an aircraft on a moving sea vessel! Well.

The church is on the corner of Station Road and Harwich Road and if you look across the latter, to the right, you will see a house called milestones and, just in front of this, well – a milestone! This shows Harwich to be 9 miles, Colchester 12 and London 63. In practice the latter is a fair bit further by road, but if you were a crow you would have to fly 63 miles.

In front of you, across the road from St. Lawrence Church is the first watering hole in a while. The Strangers Home (there must have been an apostrophe there at some point – the stranger is home? The home belonging to the stranger(s)?).

Nevertheless, this 1930s faux-timbered edifice contains food and drink. And toilets.

Past this and then Beerhouse Cottage, pass a turning for the caravan site on the left and as soon as Bradfield is seen it is over. A field is to our left and a scattering is to our right.

Little more than 50 metres past the caravan sign, wonder of wonders, just opposite the large dwelling "Curlews" is a trig-point. These four-sided stunted obelisks are redolent of the high points of the mountainous counties of the rugged north and are barely seen in the eastern counties (indeed, the highest points of Cambridgeshire, Suffolk and indeed Essex don't even bother announcing themselves with such a monument), but there it is "OSBM 10911"

A milestone and a trig-point within 100 metres of each other – an anorak's delight!

The walk now winds down Station Road for 600-700 metres, hardened footway on the right for much of the way. The very bricked Stour Lodge Cottage is of note, then Stour Lodge itself. A grassy apron opens out on the right and a thin blue band can once more be seen.

As the grass reaches its widest point near the Elmsworth House B&B a glad bench is offered up, angled towards the fields and the mighty river. Next to this a posy and the cut-out shape of an ewer in remembrance of someone lost.

A nearby gate serves a field with a horsebox and enviable views of the Stour, lucky whoever. This is just a place for us to linger though as we sweep down the hill towards the river (losing views of it though, as the land falls). Down the hill a red-roofed building shows off its white face. On closer approach this is seen as a pretty cottage. This is Ship Lane and we must turn right here.

In 100 metres, having passed by two or three more dwellings, narrow Ship Lane disappears in to trees and then under a railway bridge and deliciously near to the Stour, which should soon be with us for a long time. 200 metres of path, to the right of the trees, and our views of the salty estuary re-appear.

For the next three miles we will be walking by the water.

The views, and the close-up experience are pretty much as one would expect of Essex' northern coasts once away from the golden beaches – muddy, creeky inlets, saltmarsh, the skeletons of long-dead boats.

Half a mile along, though, the mud gives way to the sand as we approach Jacques Bay (remember Squadron Commander Edwin Harris Dunning DSC RN of Jacques Hall fame? He was from hereabouts).

The path does occasionally tuck inside a group of trees, but generally is coastal. All is quiet. A mile until the first house, Ragmarsh Farm, a Georgian affair, with a sumptuous front lawn and stunning views across the estuary.

Wrabness Nature Reserve takes the tarmac path away from the water and in to the woods, with its hides, but that is only a short distraction as the views open up again and the colour yellow presents itself. These are the sand cliffs well known of the east coast, perhaps in Dunwich more than most, where this soft crumbling mineral has caused the land to be eaten away.

The path moves on and 100 metres from the woodland crosses a bridge over a slender inlet, one of those which weaves what appears to be an ephemeral path through the soft mud which somehow survives the slings and arrows of the tide.

About 80 metres past the bridge there is a confluence of paths. The public footpath is shown to go off to the right. From here it marches on for 700 metres on a field edge before heading left and back towards the coast.

However, it is possible (depending on the tide) to instead turn left and locate some concrete steps and find again the river. Apparently, the beach is private here, although that is not immediately apparent. It is commonly held that only from the high-water mark can there be "ownership". In any event, there is certainly no problem in being here a while, still less just passing through. Of course, if tide is up, revert to public footpath (which, by the way, hits a private lane after 150 metres, turning left on which would get you back towards the water).

Time to take a closer look at those sandy cliffs. Geologically these tell the passing of the ages, thin definable bands of sand over 50 million years. Pale at the bottom, richer at the top for the soil from today's vegetation. On a later stretch of cliff, several bands of volcanic ash are in view, apparently caused by Scottish volcanoes. Famous finds amongst these cliffs include a mammoth in 1701

These cliffs are quoted as being the highest vertical cliffs in Essex (up to 16 metres) although those at Walton-on-the-Naze must surely rival them. They are, of course, in constant flux, the waves ever beating at the lower levels, the wind whispering away the little particles, the sea always winning.

Unwittingly helping the sea are the Sand Martins. A dun coated black and white-winged relative of the inhabitants of gables *Riparia riparia* have pitted the cliff walls with holes for nests and can be seen, flitting gregariously in the spring and summer into and out of their straw-bedded tunnels.

Even from afar, it would not have escaped notice that a lofted wooden structure sits just beyond the sandy cliffs. This, of course, is nothing more or less than a beach hut. As we round the headland it becomes apparent that there is quite a little group of them, about 50 all-told (#42).

These tackle the problem of the in-coming water by being built on stilts

Some of these creations are very large indeed, containing several rooms and wholly worthy of accommodation, although cannot, must not (should not!) be lived in. The attractiveness of so doing is clarified in a recent advertisement for one of the "chalets" further on, selling for £170,000 where the estate agent stated: "the huts have no mains electricity, water supply or sewerage. Hut owners typically use bottled gas for cooking and solar power if applicable, wind power and/or 12-volt batteries for lighting. Fresh water for drinking is available from stand pipes typically from April through to October or of course owners bring their own supplies."

Then is a stretch of a couple of hundred metres where the huts are fewer and none, trees climb up on the right, their rooted feet both binding and clawing at the crumbling soil. A warning sign speaks of danger and advises that a nearby path that had once been there is no more.

As the little wooden holiday houses run out, a footpath sign is seen and the white drums first seen down Manningtree way are ever closer. The path reaches slightly to the right and will take us south-east, shaving off a triangle of land that is little more than marsh.

We are now back on the Essex Way as we pass a caravan park on our right, small trees on our left shelter us from the desired views (which also contain a last few stray beach huts) for a hundred metres or so.

As the views do open up again, we pass Shore Farm on the right and the land is banked up on a field edge. Over to the right is the first glimpse of a minaret-style roof, out-of-keeping with the flat lands of Anglia. And the path winds on, disappearing amongst trees, over to the right again that minaret, not so much a minaret, a pair of steep-sided gables, one small one bigger, decorated in Byzantine patterns.

The path now approaches thicker woodland and as it reaches the gates of the forest there are two options: straight on (for that is the way we are headed) or to the right. The latter option takes us to Wrabness Station, which may be the desired endpoint of a foreshortened day, it also takes us to the community shop (as the sign informs us), but it also takes us to that unusual-looking building. A detour of 250 metres – and it's worth it.

This is "A House for Essex" otherwise known as "Julie's House" and what an architectural gem! This was designed by the artist and writer Grayson Perry in collaboration with architect Charles Holland and opened in 2015. It is available for hire and by all accounts well worth it for the bells and whistles which are inside as well as out.

From here the station is a further 250 metres, over the railway line, past the community shop and then around on the right.

If you're in it for the long haul though, turn about and head over that little wooden bridge right into the woodland for 100 metres. For the next 250 is a treelined field edge with gaps giving views of the shimmering, this is Copperas Bay. To the right, views are no less special, rolling farmland, Stour Wood beyond.

All is most lovely; all is much like the other side of the river. That is AONB, this is not and it is unclear why. It is not easy to put to bed the notion that it was simply because of the county in which it is found. Anyway, moves are afoot to change that and quite right too.

Simon Amstutz, Manager of the Suffolk Coasts and Heaths AONB team has confirmed that, finally, after more than twenty years of preparation, the matter is almost satisfied. All that is required now is the signature of the Secretary of State – watch this space in 2020!

But what will the expanded AONB be called? "Suffolk and Essex Coasts and Heaths" has been touted, but you can guess where the opposition to that has come from (!)

Soon is a full-height kissing gate and a planked footbridge and we pass by a beautifully manicured lawn, part of a luxurious landholding. This is Strandlands, four acres of garden which is occasionally open to viewing. If nothing else, you can see a little of it from the footpath.

Strandlands and another full-height kisser!

When the views to the left do open up, the most striking feature is the Royal Hospital School at Holbrook about two miles away. Through another full-height kissing gate and over another plank bridge, views of the Stour open and they close. If Holbrook is of note to the left, then to the right must be mentioned the cranes as the ports of Harwich and Felixstowe heave in to view.

Half a mile from Strandlands, the path steps down onto a wooden bridge and enters once more the kingdom of the trees. This is the Stour Estuary Nature Reserve, declaring itself to boast internationally important numbers of grey plovers, knots, redshanks, dunlins, pintails and black-tailed godwits. Nightingales, bullfinches and song thrushes are also hereabout.

Not far in, the path forks slightly left and in a while crosses another of those funny little footbridges and just 400 metres in to the woods, we must bid farewell to the west-east path and turn right and south over the railway line, taking a sombre concrete padded bridge, flanked by severe black engineering bricks. There is a sign to a car park and another telling us that we are in Copperas Wood Nature Reserve.

The path dances among the trees, just hugging the western edge of the wood for about 300 metres, a tennis court to the left being the first signs of renewed civilisation.

Now another sign ups the ante, apparently Copperas Wood is a SSSI (Site of Special Scientific Interest). Soon enough though, a field gate tells us that it's all over. We are on the B1352 Wrabness Road. Turning left, this is our "footpath" for the next 350 metres and is best trod on the right-hand side to begin with, then left onto a greensward as the bushes take over on the right. We pass the wrought iron gate of a big house called.... Copperas.

What exactly *is* Copperas?

Iron II Sulphate known since ancient times as Copperas and as Green Vitriol is, in its hydrated form, used medically to treat iron deficiency, and also for industrial applications.

The copperas industry was important in eighteenth century Essex. This involved the gathering of pyrite nodules (or 'copperas stones') from beaches, where they had been washed out of the London Clay, then allowing them to oxidise for several months in open vats. This process converted the nodules to ferrous sulphate (or green vitriol), which was an essential chemical for making dyes, ink, and several industrial chemicals such as sulphuric acid.

This has been described as the world's first industrial chemical process - a good century before the "Industrial Revolution". Wives and children of fishermen were employed to gather the nodules from the beaches and were paid in copperas tokens.

Well there you go then.

About 150 metres past said house and just opposite a sign for the entrance to.....Copperas Wood Cottage! a footpath on the right takes us back to the fields. 600 metres of field-edge due south, then left (east) for another similar amount will get you to the village of Ramsey. Sign posting for the Essex Way (although, at the time of writing at least one of the way-markers had fallen over) should lead you there.

But if they don't, something else will.

Bless me if there is not a windmill – sails and all! And we are headed exactly towards it.

The second part of this section sees us divided from horses on the right by a six-foot-high post and rail fence Another kissing gate and a last stretch of path cuts through the crop to the mill.

The Ramsey Windmill (#43) was originally built in Woodbridge, dating back to 1838 and was moved here in 1842. This is a Grade II* listed post mill – a post mill is one where the entire body of the mill is mounted on a vertical post so that the blades can turn to face the wind. It is three-storeys high, in common with the Suffolk family of mills it once belonged to.

Incredibly this mill was still working up until the second world war before neglect was followed by restoration in the 1970s and further restoration in the last few years.

The mill is now a private dwelling with a horse-riding school attached to it. On the path we have taken you are separated from it by a fence, but can get up close and have a damned good view.

Day Four Part Four

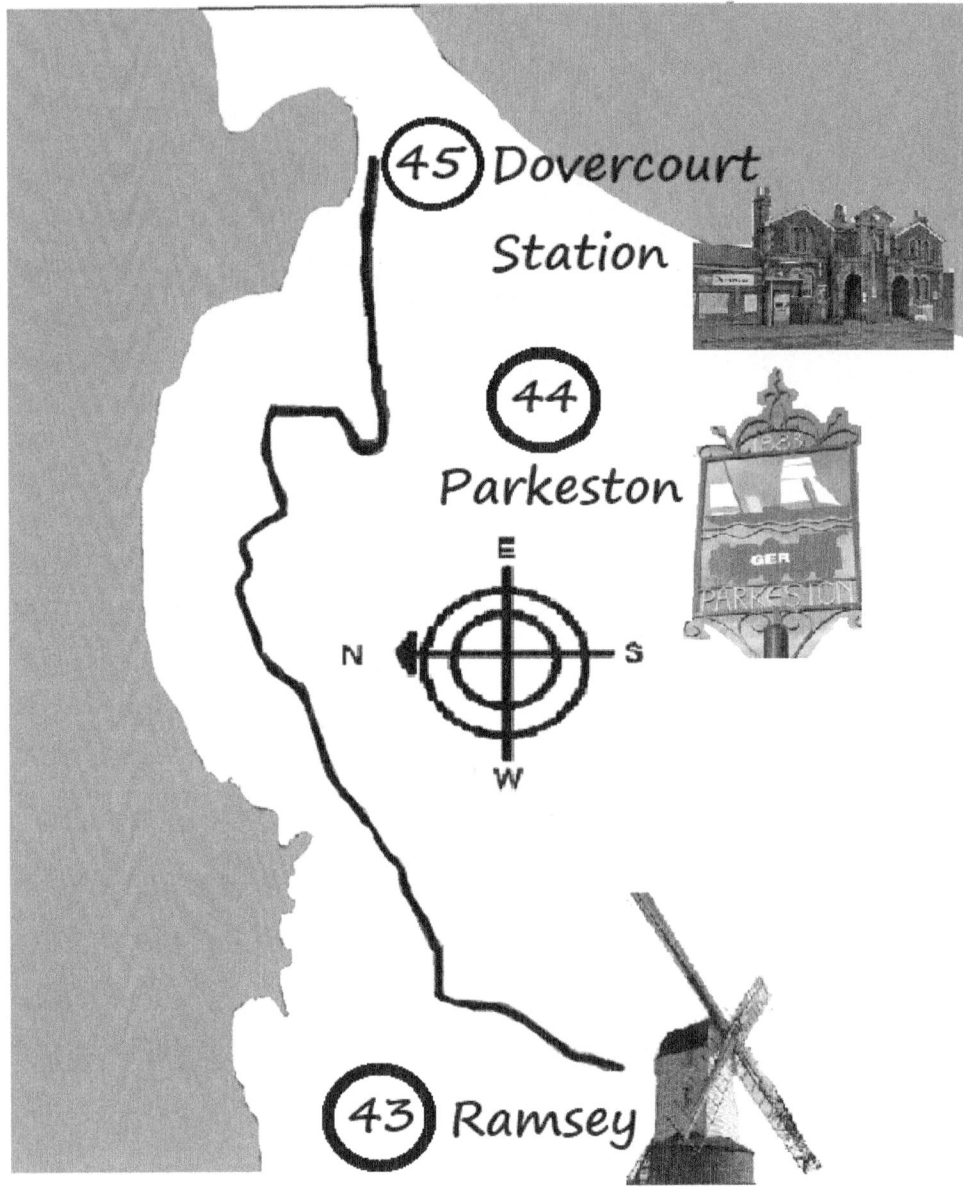

Turning right at the mill, the path is hemmed in between trees to the right and a timber fence to the left (with, by the looks of it, some low current animal deterrent). Ahead the cranes of Harwich grow ever nearer.

For 60-odd metres this is so, before the path turns hard right and the confinement becomes even more, well, confined, a choice between vegetation and barbed wire on which to ensnare yourself. This stretch goes by gardens on the right for 100 metres and we then stumble upon a 19th century Methodist-looking brick building. A plaque on the front confirms it as a Wesleyan School.

Squeezing between this and a cream-rendered property, one emerges on to a charming little street, in fact The Street, dotted with older mansarded one and-a-half-storey dwellings, mixed with one or two newer ones. It is the newer which win the day a little later on and it is of continued frustration that such ill-fitting arbitrary buildings are allowed amongst what would have been visual delight – humble cottages next to rows of nothing good, the exquisitely-composed The Gables, somehow making rough-render and panelling work with red-brick through considerate fenestration, string courses jettied sections and splayed arches; that opposite a squat buff-brick bungalow and bland 1970s nothing house, oh the disappointment.

But up the road is a pub.

Yes, just 200 metres from the Wesleyan School (irony) is the Castle Inn. At the time of writing this was undergoing renovation – for continued use thank God. No drink today, but next time…

At the end of The Street is a triangle (paved this time, not grass) and we turn left, leaving The Street and happening upon, would you believe it? That Wrabness Road again.

The housing is of more modern stock as we peel away from the historic core, one even boasts the amusing name "Prosecco Palace." Then an historic building on the left is seen.

This is red brick, and odd amalgam of the ages. Symmetrical, possibly Georgian, on the left, mansarded with a first-floor bay window in the middle and a pan-tiled, single-storey, stable-type of range on the right. The fenestration, especially on the left, gives it an olde shoppe feel. The name "The Lord Nelson" is a give-away – alas, a long time no more a pub.

Soon after is a wide greensward on the left, and on the right the view opens out to fields and those little white picket fences show themselves, bidding traffic to slow down.

To the right of these is a footpath sign and this will be our route, across the fields, for the next 500 metres. With hedging on the right, at the point it peeks out in to a new field, with trees on both sides, whilst the footpath is shown to go left then right, it is also possible to turn right and reach a little watercourse

(Dovercourt Dock River) following this for a good 400 metres until the path veers away from it and we come out on to little Ray Lane.

Turning right by a field gate and following a dusty path, we are about 200 metres from our river, soon narrowing down to little more than 50. However, 500 metres on, it is not the Stour-cum-sea that confronts us, but instead the cruel gates of industry. A sign warns of dire consequences for removing oil without paying duty and suddenly we are upon those giant white drums.

These beasts vary in size and are from five to thirty-five metres across, but oddly soothing through their perfectly smooth circularity. The walk from one end to the other is about 400 metres and with two-metre high iron pailings between us and them is not the most salubrious stretch of the Stour. There is some relief to the right with views of a golf course, but with rolling stock to the left, there is a general feeling of industry having the last word with just two miles until the end of it all.

A

sombre brick building on the right, followed by a portacabin and functional DSV building, and as the buffers are seen on the left, the analogy lingers. Iron mesh fences, Refinery Road, is that all there is? This is Harwich International – the place you use if you're getting a boat – nowadays just to the Netherlands.

Signage for passenger and cruise terminals, for car ferry terminals. Nothing for us walkers, it feels like we probably shouldn't really be here. Refinery Road swings around to the right to become West Dock Road and there is, at least, a thin path on the left-hand side, next to the hundreds of parking spaces.

Our river, in its full fury, is over-left. It can be sensed rather than seen, thanks to the far bank and the floating traffic. If we followed West Dock Road to the end (about 400 metres) we would happen upon a security control point – amazingly this is still the designated public footpath; 200 metres more until the railway terminus of Harwich International Station and the departure buildings and the ships themselves. This is no place to go for a stroll, unless you're getting a boat.

So, wind back, West Dock Road. 80 metres since you joined it is a turning on the right (Foster Road) then within yards turn left on to Station Road. Taking the thin left-hand path, pass the crucifix and the little church of St. Pauls. On the right is the Energy Skills Centre of Harwich (whatever that is). Station Road is a long, tree-lined road with not much to mention, but we are now approaching the built-up part of Parkeston (#44), which will feed in to Harwich. There are a number of ways to pick our way through, the best is to find a place to eat perhaps? Or just a drinkie?

200 metres down on the left, by a new but geometrically bland edifice, is Garland Road. This is largely residential, of modest turn of the century stock, features a converted church on the left (opposite Skippers the chippy on the

right) a convenience store 100 metres on from this and, of crucial importance, a pub on the right (the Fryatt Hotel and Bar).

Garland Road runs out after about 500 metres and arrives at a village sign for Parkeston and a path leading to a park. This kicks slightly to the right and runs for 100 metres before reaching a hardened footway which goes right and soon crosses the Dovercourt Dock River again.

It's fair to say that the next bit is utilitarian, 250 metres of Parkeston Bypass, taking in a roundabout and various retail outfits (including Morrisons on the left).

Once arriving at the second roundabout (the St. Nicholas Roundabout) turn right and take advantage of the pedestrian relief island to cross what is in fact the A120.

Once the other side, by Lidl and the Premier Inn/Brewers Fayre, carry on right on a thin path, protected by crash barriers. 100 metres from the crossing, we swing around left with the roundabout and take the first turning – Parkeston Road. Just 50 metres in is a little lane next to some smaller dwellings.

Left down here....

This bends right then left and for a kilometre the footpath is hidden amongst the trees finally emerging at the much be-balconied Station Lane, narrow and made yet narrower with a riot of often-trimmed bushes and overhanging trees to the left. The housing stock changes from modern flats to traditional houses, all with the same problems of precipitous driveways and tortuously narrow manoeuvring space.

Station Lane

300 metres later and we arrive at the Victorian Dovercourt Station (#45).

Day Four Part Five

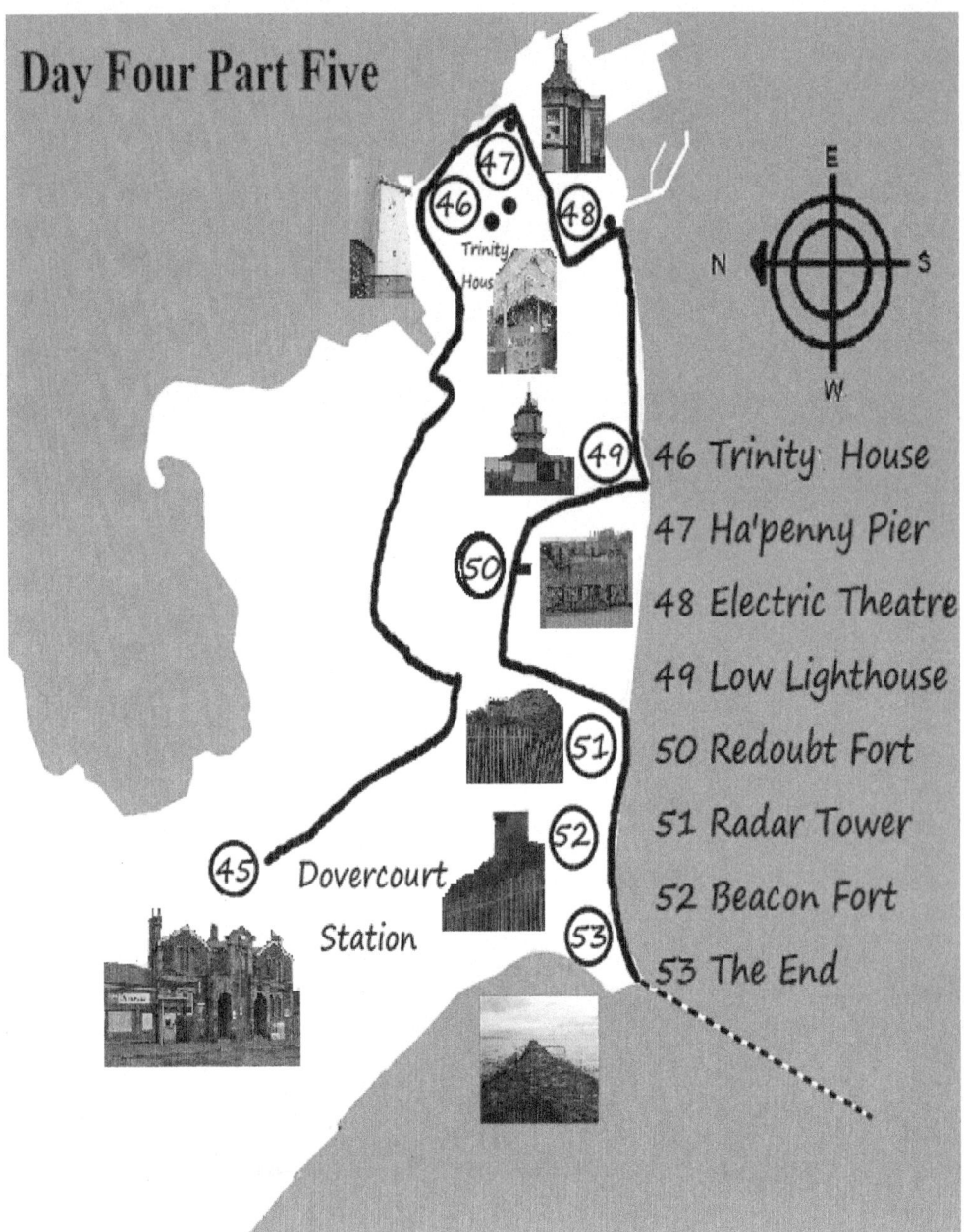

46 Trinity House

47 Ha'penny Pier

48 Electric Theatre

49 Low Lighthouse

50 Redoubt Fort

51 Radar Tower

52 Beacon Fort

53 The End

Dovercourt Station

For the last mile or so, the Stour has never been more than a couple of hundred metres to our left. However, we may as well be miles from it. Between us and it are the above-mentioned bushes, a railway line, more overgrowth, the A120 and 20-30 metres depth of alluvial wasteland. Whilst it would have been possible to walk at least the second part of this journey on a reasonably wide, if at times crumbling and precipitous, path on the riverside of the A120, this is essentially as grim as it sounds.

But we are at the station now and need to resign ourselves to about one kilometre of urban reality. Leaving the ornate station and its associated abandoned buildings (i.e. the ticket hall, everything is by machine now) behind, walk straight on along Station View and poke through on the left by the railway line and overhead bridge.

This emerges on to Grafton Road, early 20th century housing stock, punctuated by newer housing near Park Road. Then oddly flat-roofed dwellings in all manner of coloured render are succeeded by more traditional stock. We are now moving along the little peninsula only 1km long and no more than 750 metres wide – at its widest.

Just after this the road hitches around to the left and becomes Fernlea Road and all the time we are drawing nearer to the distant cranes. Eventually we want to turn left to try and re-discover the estuary. Alexandra Road is as good a turn as any, where level-crossing gates can be seen 50 metres along and the track is crossed.

100 metres along, at the end of Alexandra Road is the promisingly-named Stour Road, curling around to the right by a harsh concrete wall, metal railings, wooden fence the A120 and industrial building (showing as Telegan Pressed Products!) which at least block off views of 200+ metres of visual disappointment before the salty spume is king.

With a balustraded walk on the left, a friendly pavement on the right helps Stour Road wind its way for 500 metres north until its end. Passing Pepys Street on the right (named after Harwich's most famous son) cars spill all over the pavement as e'er they did at the Bathside Garage. 60 metres more and Stour Road runs in to Albermarle Street opposite the geometrically bland office building Haven House.

Turning left, after just 20 metres we arrive at the A120 that we last saw in Parkeston and have been avoiding. Like some parts of the Stour itself, it has calmed to a tiny trickle, an echo of its former self. Across it is again a maritime feel, masts, the other side. Crossing the road, we can see this and have a look at whatever ships are nearby. Still, though, the river is barely two miles wide.

On our left is an oddly ship-like silver building which turns out to be the HQ of Trinity House – the lifeboat people (#46)

This is George Street and ahead are ships of various kinds. Now the street is called The Quay. A pleasant walkway and memorial,,,,,,

If you're looking for somewhere to eat or drink – fill your boots (remember the walk require for the Pinkhus? It seems a long time ago now….)

On the streets to the right, within 100 metres are The Samuel Pepys, The Alma Inn (with rooms) and rooms at Swanhouse, Church Street, King's Head Street, Eastgate Street; all of these little roads into Harwich's historic core are simply lovely.

Clinging to the river though, The Quay has a promenade walk, past some buildings, some grand old, some not so, the Mayflower exhibition, the Ha'penny Pier with its café (#47). From this pier you may take the foot-ferry to Shotley or Felixstowe. Even if not, it is worth a walk up and rightwards for its full 100 metres to enjoy a close-up and personal experience of the river (although later it may be possible to get even "close up and personaler").

Just along from this is The Pier Hotel and pub. If you take advantage of all the facilities Harwich has to offer, just in this little strip, and combine them with those of Manningtree and Mistley, you really could be in a little bit of a mess right now.

As you reach said hostelry, the end of it all is just 150 metres in front of you. This is the point where it could be held that the river "ends".

However, there are two problems here:

1) This is a headland, and it could be argued that the river continues for a little way more (over one kilometre more);

2) You can't get to it anyway (this is Harwich Navyard Wharf, featuring Harwich Dock Company and Man & Son Mannlines – home to stevedoring and warehousing, Ships Agency & Cargo Forwarding and other ship-type things, but not a place to go for a stroll).

The "end" we may not see....

Therefore – by using these expedients we lap up one last bit of what can properly still be described as the Stour before it becomes the open sea.

Turning right around The Pier, Harwich as a working port can be seen for all its brutal, but job-creating and life affirming, loveliness. The buildings of King's Quay Street now shield us from this and 100 metres on there is a turning to the left ("Outpart Eastward"), offering the New Bell Inn and glimpses of the estuary.

However, by avoiding this, several gems can be enjoyed. First the Old Bank Studio (an old bank, which is now a studio – not open to the public so often, but a place for art classes – however its architecture is to cherish), opposite the sumptuous number 44, but the real jewel is just next to this, The Electric Palace (#48). This is one of England' oldest cinemas.

Old Bank Studio

The Electric Palace - under wraps!

The next building is the 1912 Centre and Bunkhouse – a place for accommodation. Turning left *here* along Cow Lane is the suggested route towards the coast. And the coast is obviously flagged up straight away, with the Lifeboat Museum on Angelgate. Picking your way through here and past Harwich Sailing Club, you are back at the river and on to a sandy beach.

This beach carries on for 200-300 metres and at the end of it, if you cast your eyes right is Harwich High Lighthouse, worth a look if you have a moment. If not, you may as well carry on the way you are going until you get to, wait for it, Harwich *Low* Lighthouse (#49). And if you walk just over 50 metres to the right of *this* and if you have any space left, there is the Café on the Green which, according to its publicity, is open all 24 hours (just not when we were there (!)).

The High ....and The Low

In fact, to take in one of Harwich's best-loved attractions, you'll have to walk in this direction anyway and abandon the shoreline for about 250 metres.

With said café on your right and moving away from the briny, carry on along Harbour Crescent with its 1930s housing stock and follow this for about 150 metres before turning left down Main Road (the B1352). Passing the synagogue (on the right) after the second block of houses you will see a blue signboard and, perchance, a pair of flags and a thin path between two dwellings. This will take you to that highlight – the Redoubt Fort (#50).

Built between 1808 and 1810, this was one of 29 Martello towers on the East Anglian coast in preparation for the Napoleonic invasion which never came. Retired on several occasions, it re-emerged as a detention centre for British troops awaiting trial and was finally used by the British Civil Defence Organisation. Restoration since the late 1960s has led to the thing before you today, impressive and worth a couple of hours if you have time.

Re-emerging on to Main Road, turn left to complete the loop, more modern flats opposite. 100 metres on, turn down Mayflower Avenue for about 250 metres until the river-walk is re-found.

Just on the right, to the left of a sign for Barrack Lane, is a cut-through to the final walk.

Even in these last 200 metres, there is still the Harwich Radar Tower (#51) and Beacon Hill Fort (#52) to mention. And then, just next to the Cornwallis Battery, there it is, the end of it all. Well, not quite.

You will have, from afar, noted a thin promontory of some length. This jetty (#53) protrudes some 450 metres in to the Stour, about one-quarter of the way across to Landguard in Felixstowe.

This is a long walk and best taken (if at all) when the tide is far out and the sea in its smallest fury. It is the closest up and most personal you can get to this mighty river short of jumping in a boat or going for a swim. If you don't fancy this last walk, no worries. There has to be an end, and this *is* where it ends.

That little bridge near Water Hall some 50 miles and four days away, the water that passed under there passes here too and the individual molecules of $H2O$ which drifted under your feet on that first day came and went by here long before you did.

That was the Stour, the southern bank of the Stour with its flat and rolling fields of Essex barley, with its flint and round-towered churches and its grand country houses, its sleepy villages and its romantic Stourside towns, of ghosts and witches.

That was the Stour they never tell you about and God alone knows why, for this is God's own country.

That was the Stour, an *Essex* river.

From the Same Author

Climb Every Mountain – (From the Nearest Pub and Back)

Coming in 2020/21

The Ghost Grounds – Discovering What Became of England's Lost Football Stadiums

The longest Path – Walking the Essex Coast

Printed in Great Britain
by Amazon